The Guard

Brazilian Jiu-Jitsu Details and Techniques: Volume 2

The Guard

Brazilian Jiu-Jitsu Details and Techniques: volume 2

Joe Moreira
&
Ed Beneville

GRAPPLING ARTS PUBLICATIONS, LLC
COSTA MESA, CALIFORNIA

WARNING:

Practice of the material in this book is inherently dangerous and could cause injury or death. Martial arts should be practiced under the guidance of a qualified instructor. Be mindful to avoid injuring yourself or others practicing the techniques in this book. The authors and Grappling Arts Publications, LLC, deny any liability for the use or misuse of the material herein. Consult a physician before engaging in the activities demonstrated in this book. Train smart.

International Standard Book Number: 978-0-9721097-4-1

Printed in China

SECOND EDITION, 2009

CREDITS

This book was conceived, written and produced by Ed Beneville and Joe Moreira. Photography by Anthony Peters and Casey Beneville. Edited by Ed Beneville with assistance from Tim Cartmell, Valerie Worthington and Kirby Beneville.

ABOUT THIS BOOK

Joe Moreira has thirty-seven years of experience in Brazilian jiu-jitsu. In this volume, he shares core elements of his jiu jitsu as well as the specific details needed to make it work. Moreira's teaching philosophy is that it is better to understand groups of moves/options from given positions than isolated moves. The idea is to show sequences of moves from specific positions so that you have a strategy to use when the scenario arises. You need to know not only how to attack or defend from a position, but also how to handle your opponent's likely reactions if your first move fails. As long as your opponent is reacting to catch up with your moves, you are leading him; you are controlling where the battle goes. If you know where the battle is headed, you will be in a better position to capitalize when it gets there. This volume provides a number of different games to play from the guard position. It is not an attempt to cover all things guard.

Again and again, the games involve mounting an attack and then countering defenses to it right away. Jiu jitsu is physical chess. As in chess, the ability to see multiple moves ahead of the current situation is key. Unlike in chess, the moves unfold at a rapid pace, there are not breaks between moves, and you don't have to wait for your opponent to finish his move before continuing with your next move. If you know a game well enough to transition from one move to another without having to stop and think, your chances of success with it improve considerably.

BJJ is a dynamic art in which any given starting point presents multiple options leading to multiple possible reactions and so on and so on. BJJ is based upon principles of leverage and positional dominance. Before you can get a submission you must first be in position: **first position then submission**. Fundamental to positioning is core body movement and, in particular, hip movement. Hip movement is at the heart of BJJ and is emphasized in this volume. The book begins with chapters on fundamentals and defense. After that, however, do not feel constrained to follow the order of the chapters. It may make sense to skip around depending on your interests, needs, style, and preferences.

As with volume 1 (*Passing the Guard*), this book is picture-intensive. Though this book is geared toward visual learning, do not neglect the text. There are valuable nuggets of information within the text that describe details that may not be readily apparent from the pictures alone. Most of the material is shown from multiple angles. This is necessary to see clearly what is going on and to provide perspective. The pictures are laid out to make it easy for the eyes to follow the progression of the techniques. Typically, where there are multiple camera angles, the alternate views appear one on top of the other. In some cases, the different angles were photographed simultaneously, in others not. Do not get hung up on slight differences in the position of the subjects from one camera angle to another.

Many of the photos are illustrated. The illustrations are meant to highlight key details. Sometimes the highlighted items are discussed as part of the accompanying text and sometimes not, but they are always significant. Also, the pictures depict much that is very important but that is not discussed or highlighted. There are two different colors of tatame in the photos. Pay attention to the movement of the subjects relative to them to get a better sense of the movements, angles, and distances involved.

All of the techniques in this book work, but none of them works if executed poorly. The difference between the success and failure of a technique sometimes comes down to a single detail. Do not give up on a technique because you are not immediately successful with it. It may be that you have neglected something, your timing is off, or your opponent is a step ahead of you. First and foremost, check your positioning. Secondly, consider your training partner's reactions and resistance. For instance, if you are attempting a sweep designed to work when the opponent is driving forward, it is not going to work if your training partner is leaning back.

Some techniques will work better for some players than others. This is due to a variety of factors including skill, strength, flexibility, body type, and disposition. As to flexibility, bear in mind that Prof. Moreira is not particularly supple and that all of the techniques shown can be performed with average flexibility.

This book is aimed at a wide range of skill levels. The material presented runs the gamut from basic to advanced. We hope this book provides an abundance of useful information for even the advanced player. We do assume that the reader has at least a rudimentary understanding of grappling.

Train hard, train smart, and remember that more than anything else, success in this art requires **persistence**.

ABOUT THE AUTHORS

JOE MOREIRA

Joe Moreira is a lifelong martial artist. When he was five years old, his older brother Marcos steered him into judo as a way of keeping him out of trouble. After five months of judo, he started training in Brazilian jiu-jitsu. He has continued his training ever since and is now a 7th degree black belt in BJJ and a 3rd degree black belt in judo.

Over the years Moreira was privileged to train under many Brazilian jiu-jitsu and judo greats. In BJJ, he trained extensively under Reylson Gracie and Francisco Mansur. During his early years while training at the Carlson Gracie Academy, he received instruction from Carlson Gracie, Rolls Gracie, Pinduka, and Mario Curpetino. By age 17, Moreira received a black belt in BJJ.

Moreira began his judo career under Mauricio LaCerda, who was also a BJJ black belt under Gaston Gracie. That was at the Copaleme judo club, where Moreira also learned from judo masters Milton Moraes and Jorge Medhi. Medhi in particular would be a major influence on Moreira's development. He taught Moreira to tie groups of techniques together so that if one did not work he could switch to another. At age 20 Joe went to Japan where he studied under Isao Okano. While studying in Japan, Moreira had an experience where older, smaller judoka tossed him in spite of his strength and youth. This hammered home to him the primacy of technique.

Back before there were any world or international championships in BJJ, Moreira was a 10-time champion of Rio de Janeiro. Moreira would also be a force in organizing and promoting tournaments in his homeland, including the Atlantico Sul Cup.

During his youth and into his twenties there were not yet many BJJ competitions, so Moreira competed extensively in judo. In judo he was a three time national champion in his weight division and a two time champion of South America, and he competed for his country on the international level.

Though there has traditionally been a divide between judo and BJJ, Moreira would come to synthesize the lesson learned from the two arts and his various teachers. From judo, Moreira gained power and strength. From BJJ, he gained technique, finesse and an equilibrium between the two arts which gave him a competitive advantage in both. Moreira took the best from his experiences in both arts to create his unique teaching style.

Moreira was one of the first Brazilians to teach BJJ in the U.S.A. He organized the first major international BJJ tournaments in the country, helping grow the popularity of the art. His dedication to, and passion for, BJJ continue with this volume.

ED BENEVILLE

Ed Beneville is a black belt under Joe Moreira and had been studying BJJ since 1996. Ed is the coauthor of the first book in this series, *Passing the Guard* and the third, *Strategic Guard.* Ed is an experienced competitor. He is also an attorney practicing in Southern California in the areas of business and contract litigation.

ACKNOWLEDGMENTS

The authors would like to acknowledge Helio Gracie for making BJJ what it is, along with the rest of the Gracie family. Their combined efforts in promoting the art have been phenomenal.

ED:
Thanks to my wife and family for all their support. Special thanks to my brother Casey for all of his assistance. Thanks my instructor, Joe Moreira. Thanks to all my training partners over the years including: John Bennis, James Boran, Tim Cartmell, Jason Knudson, Patrick Tasson, Kamyar Safdari, Bill Messick, Josh Gorham, Jim Dunk, Gustavo Froes, and Glen Rosen.

JOE MOREIRA:
I would like to acknowledge all my American students for the influence they have had on me and the development of my jiu jitsu. Eighteen years of training students in the United States has changed my vision of jiu jitsu and my game. From my American students I have come to a deeper appreciation of mental fortitude, determination, and conditioning. I wish to thank Daniel Darrow, Ashot Petrossian, and Alan McLaughlin for all their support. I would like to thank my training partners, Ed Beneville, Pat Tasson, Alan Goes, Mike Tomacelli, Marco Ruas, Daniel Darrow and Aaron Blake, all of whom have contributed to the evolution and development of my jiu jitsu. Thanks to South Coast Martial Arts and Iron Bodies Gym of Costa Mesa, and Evolution Cycling of Newport Beach. Thanks to my black belt comrades from Brazil: Jomar Carneiro, Marcus Vinicius, Aloisio Silva, and Marco Ruas.

❖ CONTENTS ❖

❖ LEGEND ❖

 technique starts

 technique starts - alternate view

technique ends

path turns - down and to the left

path turns - up and to the right

 path splits into two photo sequences

 two photo sequences merge

path - connects the photo sequence

path - connects alternate photo sequence

new technique continues from end of a previous technique.

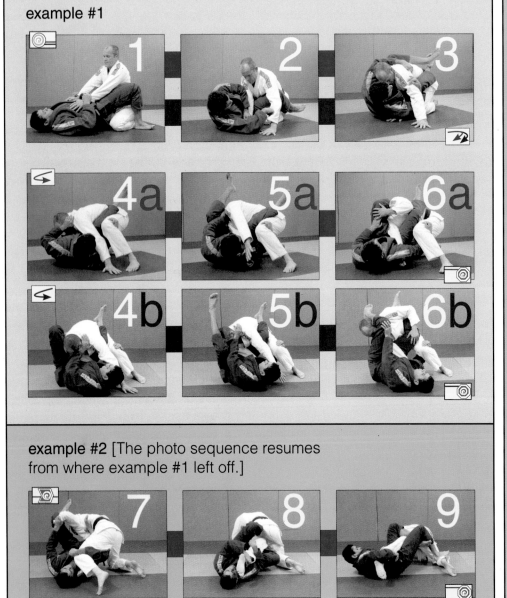

example #1

example #2 [The photo sequence resumes from where example #1 left off.]

arrows

Yellow arrows indicate Blue's movement. If a yellow arrow starts at a body part, it indicates where Blue is going to move.

If a yellow arrow ends at a body part, it indicates where Blue has just moved.

Green arrows indicate White's movement.

CHAPTER 1

SNAKE MOVES

Brazilian jiu-jitsu is a ground fighting art. Because of its nature, it involves moving on the ground using parts of the body other than, or in addition to, the feet for locomotion. Striking arts teach how to move from the feet, as does judo. In both cases, footwork is fundamental. The footwork allows the player to navigate space. So it is with ground fighting. You must be able to navigate the mat to fight effectively. But moving on the ground is very different from moving on the feet. An entirely different range of movements is possible and necessary. This set of movements is foreign to us for the most part, so it must be learned.

This chapter demonstrates a number of movements fundamental to BJJ and any other situation in which fighting off the back is a possibility. We refer to the core body movements, which entail bending/straightening and turning the hips and torso, as *snake moves*. Snake moves are also commonly referred to as *shrimping*. Every guard technique in this book involves a snake move of some sort.

The ability to move the hips is, of course, important to just about any physical activity, including walking. We all know how to move our hips to some extent; that is a requirement of day-to-day living. The body movements that make BJJ effective are not, however, something that one becomes familiar with without spending time on the mat. That being the case, practice of the snake moves, and lots of it, is in order.

Practicing snake moves is the closest thing BJJ has to the kata or forms found in traditional martial arts. That is not to say that practicing snake moves is kata, but it does serve some of the same purposes. Repeating physical movements ingrains neurological pathways that can be retraced with less and less concentration as they become well worn. As adults, we no longer have to think much about how to walk, but at one time we did. Learning the core body movements shown throughout this book is analogous. Repetition develops coordination.

Practice, and remember that perfect practice makes perfect. Learn to do the movements correctly and purposefully, and the foundation for excellent jiu-jitsu is laid. Seek to continually refine the movements; you may find room for improvement for years to come, and that is all right. It is a long journey to a point where one need no longer refine one's core body movements. Keep a steady pace down that path. Your game can only ever be as solid as the foundation upon which it is laid.

Jiu-jitsu is to a large extent a matter of maneuvering into positions from which you can:

1) pit your large muscle groups against the smaller muscle groups of your opponent; and/or,
2) use leverage/mechanical advantage in the application of force.

For instance, with the basic armbar (Ch. 5), you pit the power of your back and upper legs against the strength of your opponent's elbow (large muscle groups vs. smaller muscle groups) and position your hips so as to create a fulcrum below the opponent's elbow, using his own forearm as the lever (mechanical advantage). The key to positioning and leverage, time and time again, is hip movement. Snake moves are techniques for moving the hips.

In this chapter, applications of the various snake moves are shown after solo demonstrations of the techniques. These applications are essentially defenses to guard passes. They are, at the same time, entries into sweeps and submissions. The applications shown in this chapter only scratch the surface of what is possible. Understand the principles involved, and many other applications will become apparent with experience.

All of the techniques demonstrated in this chapter can and should be practiced as drills. Use them as drills both to develop skill and to warm up.

❂ Hip movement is at the core of Brazilian jiu-jitsu. You must become proficient at moving and turning using the power of the torso. Here is one of the most fundamental body movements for jiu-jitsu. We refer to it in this volume as the *snake move*.

Here, turning to the side creates space for freeing the bottom leg against a mounted opponent. The width of your hip bones holds up an opponent sitting on them. Your legs being thinner, space appears. Making space is a fundamental concept that we will visit time and time again.

❂ Blue keeps his elbows close to his body. Blue will use them to push, especially when using the move against a mounted opponent. But it is his torso and not his arms that will do most of the work.

 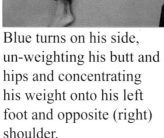  

▲ As the demonstration begins, Blue is flat on his back. The very first thing he does is raise one knee.

Blue turns on his side, un-weighting his butt and hips and concentrating his weight onto his left foot and opposite (right) shoulder.

His left leg is bent as the move begins and straightens as he pushes off the toes and pivots on the shoulder.

Blue pushes with his left foot and pivots on his right shoulder. He moves his hips toward his head. Simultaneously, his head moves in a forward arc.

⊘ All of the techniques demonstrated in this chapter can and should be practiced as drills. Repeat the moves back and forth along the length of the mat.

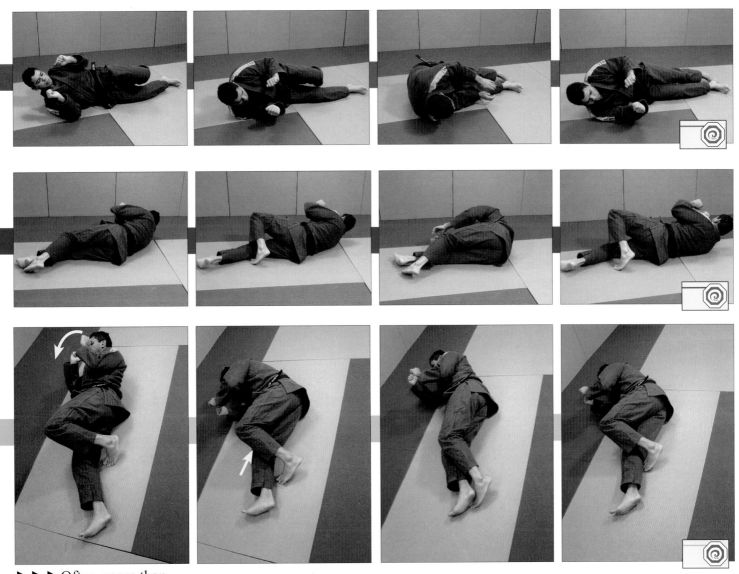

▶▶▶Often, more than one snake movement is needed to make enough space to escape or to apply a technique. Blue practices repeating the move to one side.

❷ Here is the basic snake move in action. White is about to pass Blue's guard and establish side control. Blue makes his snake move to create space for his bottom leg to go under White. Creating space by turning sideways is a movement that plays a role in many techniques. It is efficient in part because your bone structure provides a physical brace. Here, the brace comes from the planted foot and the hips. This is an example of using a mechanical advantage. Awareness of mechanical advantages will open your eyes to myriad possibilities.

White is well on his way to passing Blue's guard. If Blue does not go while White is still giving him space, he will have to work much harder to get away. Blue begins to turn to his side.

Blue pushes off his outside foot and pivots on his opposite shoulder. By turning to his side and moving away, he will create space to slide his bottom leg under and across White's torso.

Blue uses his arms ▲ to keep White from following his hips and/or ▲ to keep White from moving his hips toward Blue's head. Though his arms are involved, Blue's hips are doing the real work; the technique is not about upper body strength.

The bottom knee comes through first.

With the knee to the side, Blue has a purchase from which to help him snake his hips back under White, putting White back in the guard.

Note how Blue finishes by putting his feet in the hips and pulling on White's elbows. This flattens White out, temporarily nullifying any attack.

❂ Blue could also have locked his feet for closed guard or put his hooks in for butterfly guard.

❂ If your opponent tries to control you or pass the guard by wrapping up your legs with his arms, prevent him from controlling your upper body by keeping him away with your arms. Sometimes a strong opponent might stick you to the point where you are unable to make your snake move. Maintain some pressure of your own with your arms. Your opponent will need to loosen his grip on your legs to progress. When he does, the chance to move your lower body appears.

❷ Blue snakes to one side and then the other. You must become proficient at snaking to both sides. You do not always get to dictate the position you are in. A good habit is to drill techniques to both sides.

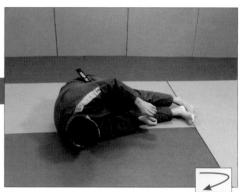

One knee is up, the arms are bent, and the elbows are close to the body. Blue makes a habit of not unnecessarily exposing his arms.

Blue turns to the side and concentrates his weight to his right shoulder and opposite (left) foot.

Blue pushes off with his foot and contracts his abdominals to add power to his bending at the waist. His hips have moved in the direction of his head.

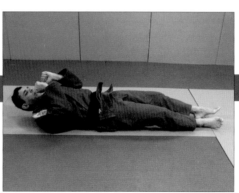

▶▶▶Blue straightens out and then repeats the move to the other side.

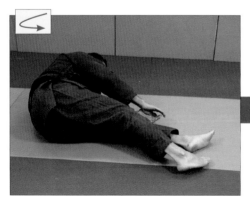

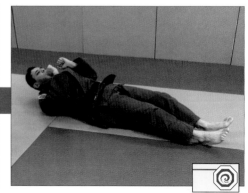

❷ Again and again, making space from bottom positions involves lifting and moving the hips by basing off a shoulder or arm and the opposite foot.

White drops his left shoulder onto Blue's abdomen.

White jumps Blue's legs and is about to establish side control.

Before he does, Blue stops him from getting any closer by snaking to his right side and blocking with his arms. Blue bridges his hips slightly and turns to his side using the space under the bridge.

By turning his hips to the side and bumping, Blue lifts White's upper body, making room for Blue's bottom (right) leg to move under White's torso, putting him back in the guard.

Blue repositions his left foot to make another snake movement.

Blue pushes off his left foot, which helps him move his hips away from White. This makes space for Blue to replace his bottom (right) leg.

Blue continues to improve his position. He breaks down White's base by using his left leg to prevent White from coming forward and at the same time raking his elbow forward.

⊚ Practice snake moves as drills. Here, for example, the drill would go like this: White moves to side control; Blue replaces the guard; Blue lets White jump to the other side; Blue replaces the guard.... Repeat the drill from one end of the mat to the other.

> ◉ Blue makes a tunnel that his bottom leg comes through. He concentrates on first turning his hips to the mat and then swinging them back toward the ceiling, pivoting on a shoulder and the opposite foot as he does.

Blue lifts his hips.

Blue turns on his side and crunches forward. He posts his weight onto his shoulder and feet.

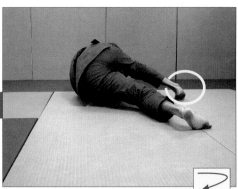

Blue steps over with his trailing foot. His hips are off the mat. He pivots on his shoulder.

Blue threads his bottom leg under the top. His weight is borne by his shoulder and his top (right) foot. He has switched his torso movement.

Blue's hips are off the mat. He pivots first on his shoulder, then his back.

Blue is back to the starting position.

Blue repeats the move to the other side.

It's all in the hips!

> ❂ Although Blue does not post on his top (left) foot in this example, the principle is the same. He uses his top (left) leg as one point of axis/base and his *opposite* shoulder as the other. With these two purchase points, he can push off and move his hips out to make space between himself and White and then turn back into the space he created. First he makes space to free his bottom leg; then he uses it to replace the guard.

White postures, preparing to pass the guard.

White puts his left palm on the inside of Blue's right knee and pushes down.

White brings his right knee across. Blue halts White's progress by pushing into White's upper body.

This gives Blue just enough space to put in his left knee.

Blue wants to move his hips out to the side to free space for his bottom leg.

Blue pushes off with his leg and, as he does so, pivots on his shoulder and to his back.

His bottom leg is now free, and it goes into White's hip to keep him from coming forward.

Blue fixes his top leg; he does not want White lying on the outside of his knee. White is off base and vulnerable to attack.

© Here is another instance of the *cross-over snake move*. Instead of coming over Blue's right leg, White comes under Blue's left leg. Once again, Blue pivots on his right shoulder and uses his left leg to aid the effort. This time, however, he switches his pivot point to his right foot and continues with something similar to the basic snake move. In both cases, he rotates his hips one way and then back the other.

White uses a smashing pass and is almost in side control.

Blue keeps turning his hips, while at the same time moving them away from White.

Now that he is facing White, Blue brings his bottom knee across. With it, he can push away White's left arm and upper body.

▲ In the bottom photo sequence, Blue varies his approach. Note how he re-posts his right foot to help turn himself back under White.

Blue turns himself back under White.

Before White can establish side control, Blue keeps a bit of space between them by straight-arming White.

Blue does not want to turn his back to White.

Blue adjusts and pushes off his right foot.

Blue starts to switch his hips so that they turn back toward White.

⊙ When fixing the guard, you must make space so you can maneuver.

Blue uses all of his limbs.

Now that he has more space and is almost centered with White, he can finish the job by pushing with his right foot.

Blue brings his bottom knee all the way across, making it easy to center White.

Blue will attack from here.

> ⊙ Combining different body movements is a key to making space to escape. The more you practice, the more you learn to put the different pieces together. Here we see two snake moves used together. Typically, it is difficult to go straight to basing on the palm, so first come up on an elbow. The key and the source of power is, once again, the hips.

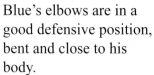

Blue's elbows are in a good defensive position, bent and close to his body.	Blue lifts his left knee.	Blue draws back his right elbow and turns to his right side. Instead of pivoting on his shoulder, he uses his elbow. He is now in a position to post on his right elbow and opposite (left) foot.	The hip movement is essentially the same as the basic snake movements. His hips move toward the space where his head had been. He moves his head to the side as he straightens his left knee.

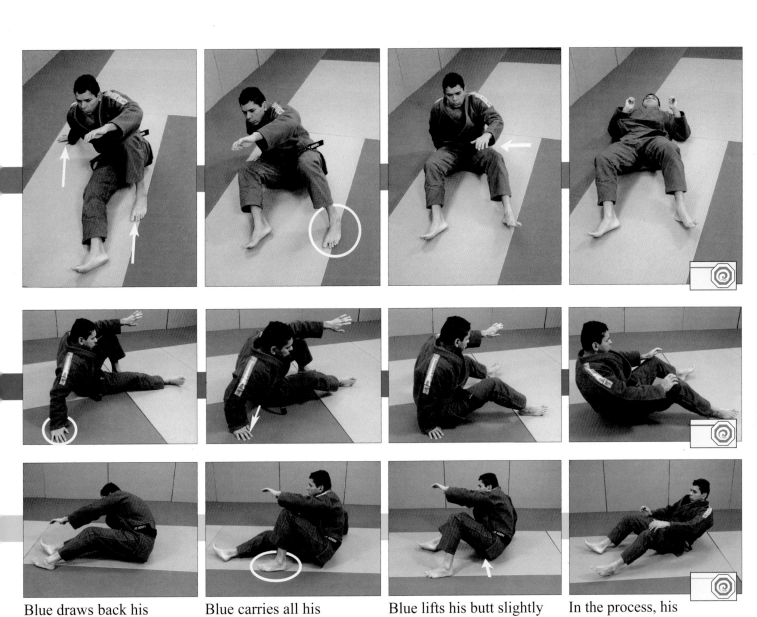

Blue draws back his
foot for the second hip
movement (top two
rows). Simultaneously,
he switches from being
on his right elbow to
posting his right hand
diagonally back.

Blue carries all his
weight on his right hand
and opposite (left) foot.

Blue lifts his butt slightly
off the mat and moves
his right hip over to his
right hand. Moving his
hips toward his posted
(right) hand makes all
the difference when an
opponent is involved.

In the process, his
body turns from being
somewhat sideways to
straight.

❷ Here, *the elbow and palm snake move* is applied. White pushes down Blue's leg and begins to come over for the pass. Blue does not wait for White to improve his position any further. Better for Blue to start before White can take away too much space.

White tries to pass by pushing down Blue's right knee and coming around Blue's right side.

A sequence of moves following from this one appears in Ch. 9: *Neck Control Attacks.*

Blue uses the space to put in his left hook. Getting this hook in is the objective of the elbow snake.

Now Blue goes up onto his elbow and onto his hand. Blue grabs White's belt. He might also grab the gi. Once on his palm, Blue snakes his hips toward that hand. This centers White and also off-balances him.

As Blue comes up onto his elbow, he pushes White's head to prevent him from following. He pulls back and posts his left foot.

The elbow snake makes it possible for Blue to use the pivoting motion of his torso to pull his trapped leg free. Blue moves his elbow in an arc so that it is a bit behind his head.

Now it is easy for Blue to come up on his elbow and pull back his hips.

Because White's head is in contact with Blue's midriff, when Blue shifts back under with the palm snake, it twists White's torso, destabilizing him.

Blue repositions both soles of his feet to White's upper thighs.

Blue finishes neutralizing the attack by pulling White's arm and blocking White's left leg with Blue's right foot.

◉ The ability to pivot on your back is critical to a good guard. The biggest key to pivoting on your back is to make the pivot point small. In other words, reduce the surface area that rubs the mat during the pivot by curving the back. Turn on an area on one side of the spine or the other.

Here; Blue pivots on one shoulder and then the other, but not both at the same time; that would create too much friction.

⊙ Once again, Blue posts on a foot and the opposite shoulder. This time he use the foot and opposite shoulder to pivot as he switches his hips. It is his hip movement that propels the move.

Hip movement, hip movement, hip movement!

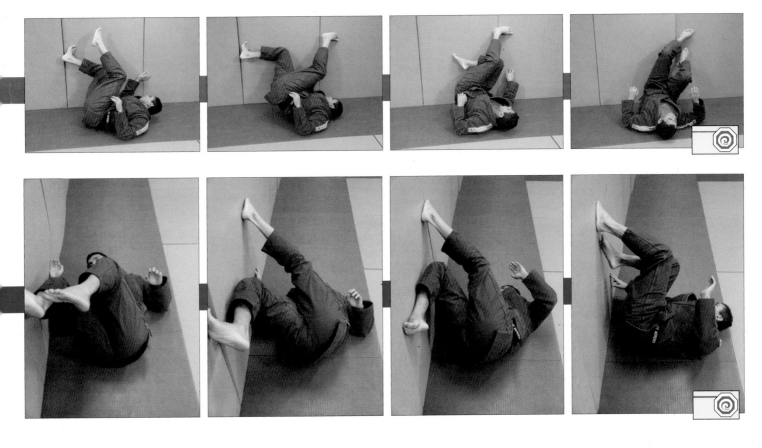

White begins to pass Blue's open guard by holding, then clearing, Blue's knees.

In the bottom row, Blue is straight-arming White's chest to preserve space.

Blue prevents White from coming chest-to-chest by using his knee to block White's hips.

As he blocks, he brings his left leg past White's head, intending to plant his foot in White's hip.

⊙ White gets further around this time so that he is over Blue's head. This forces Blue to alter his technique. Blue uses his left foot to block White, as opposed to pushing him away with it. Blue pushes White back with his right knee and fixes his feet from

Blue pushes White away with his right knee. He then puts his left foot in the space and pushes.

Once he makes White move backward, Blue swings his left leg back over White's head.

Blue puts his left foot on White's hip, and that allows him to adjust his right foot.

Blue has centered White and is poised to go on the offensive.

❷ Here again, spinning on the back is at the core of the maneuver. The smaller the area you are rotating on, the less friction you will encounter between your gi and the mat. Curve your back to decrease that area.

Blue uses his arms to gauge the distance from the wall. Blue starts by rolling backwards; he brings his legs straight over.

Blue puts the balls of his feet against the wall and pushes himself down, just a bit.

Blue picks a direction and begins to turn.

Blue pivots on his right shoulder. The balls of his feet stay more or less put, but his heels turn as his body turns.

Blue brings his head out from under his legs. His knees are bent.

Blue crosses his shins like an *X*.

Blue's head winds up on the same perpendicular line from the wall it started on.

Blue fixes his imaginary guard.

❷Sometimes the way out is to go back under. With this sort of movement, it is important to relax the knees and be sensitive to keeping good contact between the lower legs and the opponent's torso as you spin.

Another situation where Blue might have spun all the way under was shown at the bottom of pages 18-19. ▼

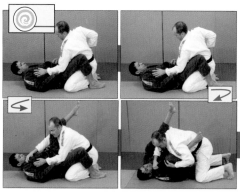 

White attempts to smash Blue's left leg to pass guard.

Blue counters by going with the flow. Because White is putting pressure on him, he will not be able to spin easily.

❷ Blue uses all of his limbs, including his head, to make this move work. Maximum efficiency involves using the whole body. Do not focus entirely on any one body part, but do not forget any either.

Blue pushes White away with his top leg. He uses both arms to turn himself.

As Blue's head completes the circle, he pushes off with his straightened arms and fixes his feet.

Note how he uses his left arm for leverage to help him snake out his hips. His head will trace a circle on the mat, first under White and then away.

Blue pushes with his right arm and pulls with his left leg.

Blue brings his right leg toward his chest to help make space to spin.

First he pushes with the right foot, and then he puts his left foot right next to it. Finally, he centers White in his guard.

Blue finishes in an attacking position.

🌀 The forward snake move is the opposite of the basic snake move. Instead of moving away from the opponent, you move toward him. Your hips move toward your feet instead of your head. Your torso crunches and then extends.

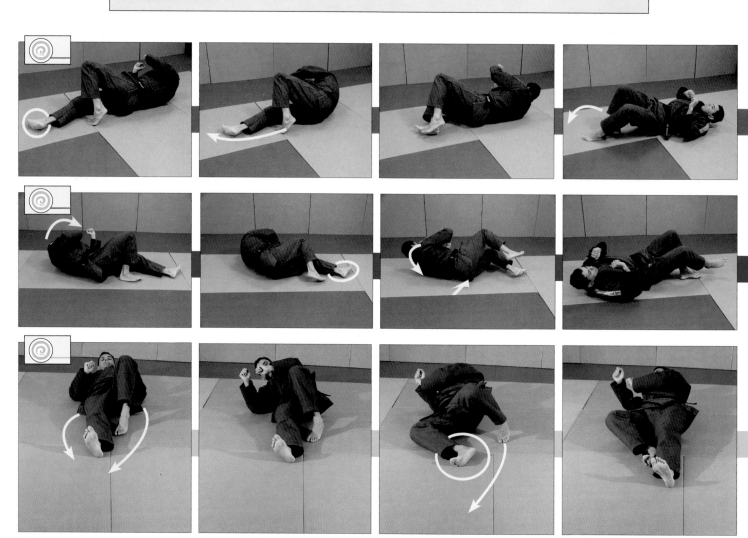

Blue posts on the outer edge of his foot, turns a bit to the side, and crunches his upper body forward.

The forward crunch allows Blue to bring his shoulder closer to his same-side foot.

Now he concentrates his weight on his shoulder and the same-side foot. This allows him to lift his hips just slightly off the mat.

With his hips un-weighted, he can now draw himself forward by both simultaneously curling his leg backward and un-crunching his upper torso.

When learning this move, try to move on the shoulder and not the elbow. Moving on the elbow certainly has its place; just not here.

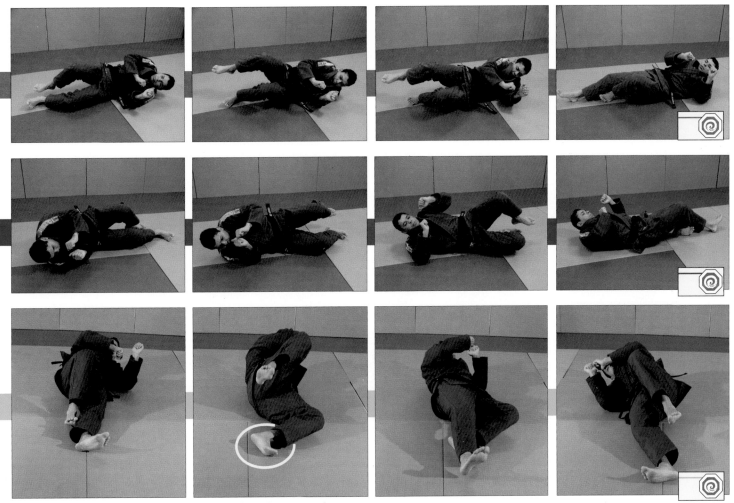

He swings his hips back under, and his torso goes from being sideways to back against the mat.

Blue drills the move by going back and forth, one side then the other.

❷ Usually, the forward snake move is used to keep the top player from backing away. Here, Blue does not want White to get away from him. As White withdraws his right leg, Blue follows, using the forward snake move. Instead of posting his left foot on the ground, as in the preceding spread, Blue hooks it behind White's retreating thigh and pulls from there.

White is backing away; Blue is losing contact and control.

Blue crunches forward and sideways. He pulls his right foot down slightly. This gives him a bit of purchase on White--not much, but enough. Blue hooks his left foot behind White's knee. That gives him a solid control point.

Blue grabs White's ankle.

⊘ The hip movement is the same as in the drill. Blue is posting/pivoting on his left shoulder. Unlike in the drill, his arms are playing an active role in pulling his hips closer.

Blue snakes his hips forward and replaces his left foot.

Blue grabs White's arm. With all four of his limbs in solid contact with White, Blue has good control for the moment.

Blue has replaced his guard. With a two-on-one grip and his feet in White's hips, Blue is positioned to attack.

At first glance, this may not look like a hip or core body movement. But it is, or at least it should be. The circular motion of the feet is assisted by keeping the hips loose and allowing momentum to generate from the hips.

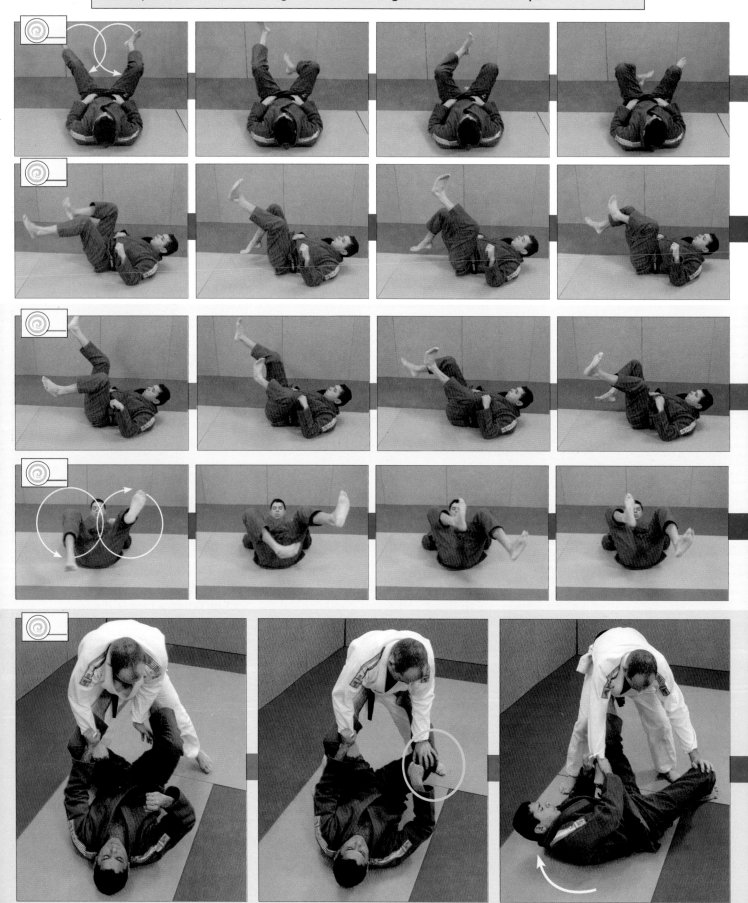

⊙ Relaxation is key to smooth motion. Be loose and fully use the range of motion of your knee joints. It is important to have a sense of one's own range of motion across the board (i.e., for all the major joints). By knowing where your foot can reach, you can judge better when to move it.

> ➋ At the bottom of the previous spread, Blue spun his knee to counter White gripping his leg. Usually it is not so easy. Here, White blocks Blue's first attempt to fix his guard, but Blue counters by switching directions. In every case, once he gets his foot in, he pushes White away.

White pushes down on Blue's knee to pass guard.

Blue posts his foot to help himself snake and to stop White from pushing further.

Blue attempts to counter by moving his foot out and up in a curve.

> ➋ This time, Blue tries first to circle his leg down and in, but White blocks the attempt by dropping his elbow. The solution is simple: Blue goes up and over.

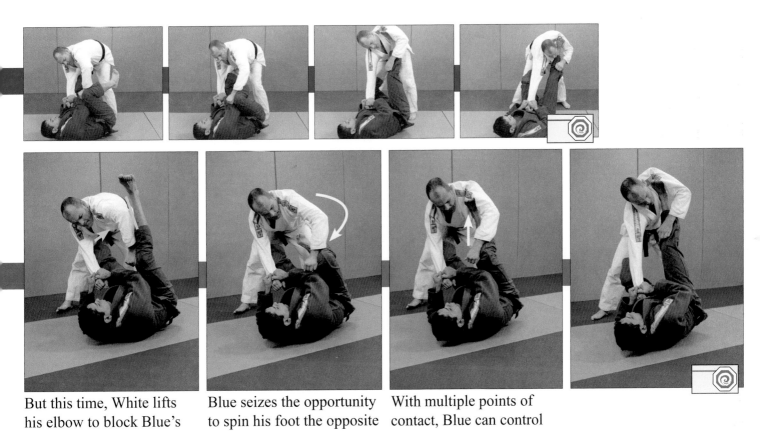

But this time, White lifts his elbow to block Blue's leg.

Blue seizes the opportunity to spin his foot the opposite way. Blue regains contact.

With multiple points of contact, Blue can control White with the guard.

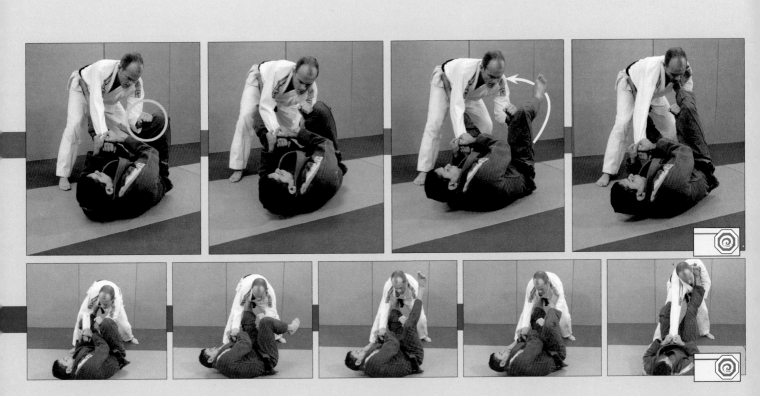

🌀 Attacks come from many directions. You must be ready to block your opponent whether he comes in high, low, or anywhere in between. Blue drills defending different levels and to both the right and the left.

 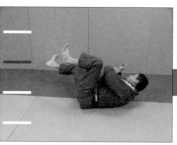  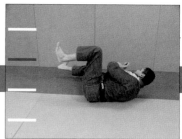

►►►►Blue drills extending his legs out from one side to another, high and low. Note that he does not lie flat on his back. He is continually a bit to one side or the other.

►►►Blue drills legwork with White. Blue does not use his hands; the drill is for the legs. White attempts to swim his arms under Blue's legs and step forward. Blue tries to prevent White from ever getting control of his legs. Blue defends by pushing White away and fending with his legs. He combines the moves shown above and the fending techniques from pages 28-31.

⊙ Blue does not lie flat on his back but rather turns his hips and goes slightly to one side or the other. His butt is slightly off the mat. Blue combines rotating his legs, straightening them, and pulling with them. The guard player does not want his opponent to have control of his legs. Blue practices techniques for preventing his legs from being controlled.

Fundamentals: Snake Moves

◉ *Moving the body core, especially the hips, is fundamental to grappling.*

◉ *Practice snake moves as individual and partner drills.*

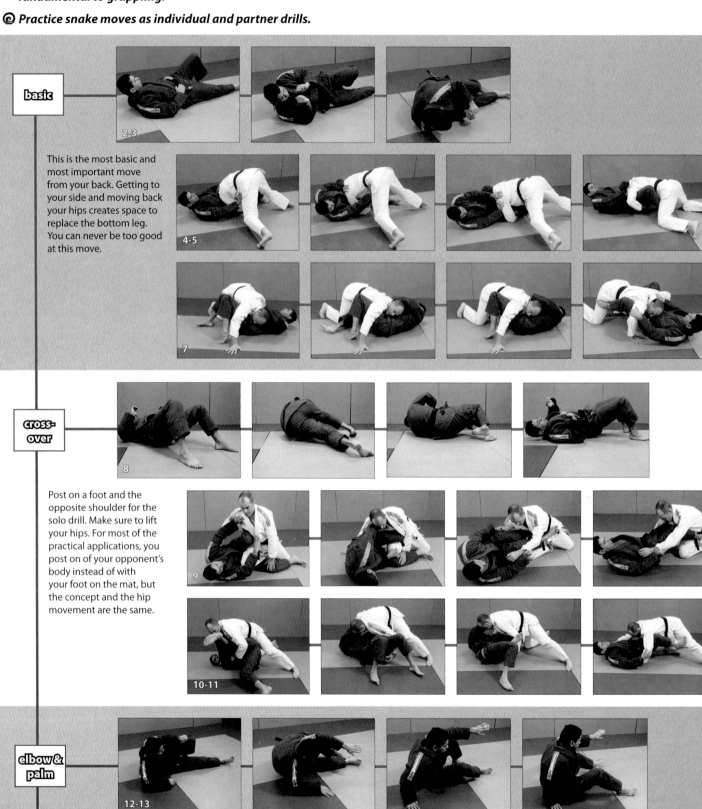

basic

This is the most basic and most important move from your back. Getting to your side and moving back your hips creates space to replace the bottom leg. You can never be too good at this move.

cross-over

Post on a foot and the opposite shoulder for the solo drill. Make sure to lift your hips. For most of the practical applications, you post on of your opponent's body instead of with your foot on the mat, but the concept and the hip movement are the same.

elbow & palm

Getting up on your elbow allows you to move your hips further than if you post on your shoulder. From the elbow you can get to your palm, giving you even more options.

cross-guard

Brace with your arms as you bring the inside knee in, then push with it. The outside leg goes around their head and the foot goes on their hip. Push with both legs to make space to fix the guard.

Use the legs to spin on your back and realign your guard. As you spin your legs, maintain a barrier between yourself and the opponent. Spin on your upper back and keep the pressure off your neck.

forward

The forward snake move allows you to move your hips closer to, or under, your opponent's. That comes in handy when he wants to back out, but you want him in the guard.

leg circles

Do not let your opponent control your knees. Circle your legs to allow yourself to adjust your feet and nullify dangerous grips on your knees.

change levels

Your opponent may attack from high or low. Practice blocking with your legs from a variety of levels. Parry your legs to find good places to put your feet.

> ❂ Here is a quick look at a few more core body movement techniques that will appear later in the volume.

BACKROLL (CH. 10)

SNAKE TO KNEES (CH. 11)

SNAKE TO STANDUP (CH. 11)

CHAPTER 2

SOME THOUGHTS ON DEFENSE

Defensive techniques can be put into three categories according to your opponent's progression: *early*, *on-time*, and *late*.

Early defenses stop attacks or guard passes as they emerge. Early defenses tend to be simple and take less energy. A good deal of early defense is simply keeping yourself in good position and off-balancing your opponent. The downside to making early defenses is that they can get in the way of mounting an offense. On the other hand, an attack itself can be a form of early defense.

On-time defenses are those between the early and the late ones. The applications shown in *Ch. 1* are, for the most part, on-time defenses. Usually you still have multiple options if you act in time, which is a good thing. Most defenses fall into this range.

Late defenses are typically last chance defenses. Either you go for it and make a successful defense or lose the position, or worse yet, you get tapped out. Avoid having to use last-chance defenses as much as possible, but don't hesitate when the time comes—and it will come.

General principles to keep in mind while defending against guard passes include:

Keep contact. Keep contact with your opponent with at least three of your limbs (not counting your head) and most of the time with four. There are a lot of exceptions to this rule, so don't get hung up on it. But even with the exceptions, you typically still need to keep contact between 3 or 4 of your limbs and the guard passer. In the case of only having contact with three limbs, the fourth is typically pushing or posting off the mat for purposes of changing position, e.g. the basic snake move.

Use everything. We have made a point so far of emphasizing core body movements. But that is only the beginning. You need to use all of your limbs. Your head is one of those limbs. It is the heaviest part of your body, and it plays a huge role in generating momentum, as when you want to spin on your back. Your head can be used to control and is a prime target for your opponent to use in controlling you, so physically use it. Do not

be inactive with any of your other limbs. If any of your arms or legs are not doing something to help, you are most likely doing something wrong.

Use your feet like hands. Think of your feet as hands, especially when the soles of your feet are against your opponent. Also, unlikely as it may sound, curling your toes forward or back is sometimes the difference between a successful and an unsuccessful technique.

Make space. A lot of guard passing involves controlling the chest and/or hips and taking away space. The corollary is that defending against being passed involves making space and keeping the chest and/or hips free.

Fight with what is free. It is very difficult for the guard passer to control the legs, hips and upper torso at the same time. It is not so difficult to control one or the other. Recognize which parts of your body are being controlled and which are free. Look for what you can do with what is free. For instance, if your opponent has his arms wrapped around your legs, then your upper body is probably free, so keep him away with your arms (e.g., pg. 9). If your opponent is focused on your upper body, use your legs to tie him up or snake your hips.

Change it up. If your first attempt at an escape fails, your opponent is on notice and will likely be better prepared to stop it--or worse--the second time. This is especially so if he is not worried about something else. Keep your head about you, and change up your techniques. The element of surprise is particularly important against more formidable opponents.

Attack. Do not forget the old maxim: The best defense is an overwhelming offense.

Though this chapter is about counters to guard passing, the topic started with the first snake move in *Fundamentals* and continues throughout the book. The snake moves in *Ch. 1* provide most of the foundation for defending guard passes. The bulk of this chapter concerns countering perhaps the most common and reliable guard pass: the

❷ Here is an example of an *early* defense. White wants to lift Blue's leg and use a smash pass. Blue sees what is coming and stops it with mechanical advantage. Once Blue puts in his hook, it takes little effort for Blue to stop White from lifting.

White begins his pass by under-hooking Blue's leg.

Blue holds the back of White's neck.

Blue uses his left leg to hook White's. White's pass is now neutralized.

❷ Here is an *on-time* defense. White has under-hooked Blue's leg and established a collar grip for a smashing-type guard pass. Blue still has space to work with, but if he waits, that space will vanish and his options will become fewer and more difficult.

▲▼White is halfway to stacking Blue.

▲▼Blue stiff-arms White to prevent him from smashing. By pushing on White's shoulder, Blue preserves enough space to bring in his right knee.

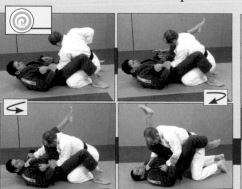

Before White can get going, Blue snakes back and onto his elbow.

🌀 This technique works best when your opponent keeps his shoulders square with you as he attempts to stack your leg.

Blue grabs White's wrist. Now he is in control.

▲▼Once he gets his knee through, Blue uses the strength of his back and leg to push White back.

▲Blue brings his knee under White's elbow and fixes his guard.

▼Blue could also bring his leg straight back.

◉ White gets too far for Blue to use the previous technique so Blue needs to try something else because White's shoulders are not square to Blue.

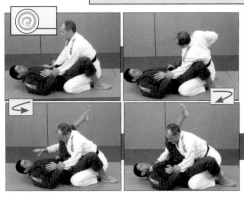

White has a good grip on Blue's lapel and is smashing Blue's knee down.

Blue is too late to stop White from smashing. Blue takes his leg off and at the same time pushes with his hands.

As soon as his right foot comes to the mat, Blue will post on it and use it to help him pull his hips away from White.

Blue bring his knee to White's right hip.

Blue pushes White away with his left leg and at the same time pulls on White's arm.

Blue straight-arms White as he moves his hips out and turns toward White.

Blue draws back his right leg and posts on the ball of his foot.

As Blue's hips turn to face White, he brings his inside (left) knee in front of White's arm.

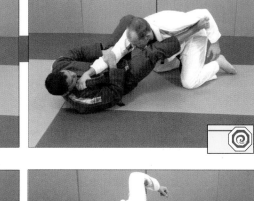

Blue continues to improve his position by pulling on White's left arm and pushing on the right arm.

Next, Blue replaces his left knee, which is in White's hip, with his left foot.

Blue is in an ideal position for a triangle attack.

❷ This time, Blue is *late* making his defense, but not quite too late. White's elbow is vulnerable to attack.

White is committed to passing to Blue's left side.

Note the angle Blue takes as he pushes. The human arm is weak at resisting force from this direction. Blue pushes White's elbow up and across.

Blue gets his knee to the outside. This fixes his guard and provides a solid control point. Blue is in a good position for attacking White's arm or taking his back. He might also just fix his guard.

Seeing an opportunity, Blue stiff-arms White's shoulder to keep him from coming forward, all the while controlling White's arm.

Blue pushes on White's elbow, turning to his side and snaking his butt under White and out.

Once Blue gets to his side, he has room to withdraw his high (left) leg.

Blue brings his left leg out and then over White's shoulder. At this point, he is relatively safe and could just fix his guard.

Blue puts his bottom (right) foot in White's hip. Now he can use both of his arms against White's left arm.

Blue extends his body and pushes with his top knee on the back of White's shoulder. Blue pulls White's arm back against the direction he is pushing with his knee.

Blue's left foot is partially hooked around White's side. This provides a little more leverage. He uses his right foot prevents White from coming forward to escape the armlock.

⊘ Here is a variation on the previous technique. Push the elbow before the opponent has a chance to smash you. In other words, go while there is still enough space between your chest and his for you to maneuver.

If possible, Blue wants to get White's elbow before White gets his collar grip.

Blue's left palm is under the inside of White's right elbow.

After his knee comes out behind White's shoulder, Blue will pull White's arm.

Blue scoops his right arm in front of White's arm.

Blue's left fist in White's right elbow keeps things tight while Blue moves his left knee into place on top of White's shoulder.

Once Blue is on his side and is pushing the elbow, there is nothing preventing him from snaking his backside out from under White.

The space created allows him to move his leg from one side of White's shoulder to the other as he pushes White's elbow.

White has to let go of his right hand grip or his shoulder gets cranked.

Blue keeps pressure on the top of White's shoulder as he brings his leg over.

Once White's shoulder is low, Blue brings his left foot in front of White's face.

For the submission, Blue squeezes his knees and uses his top (left) leg to push into White's face.

⊘ This time, after Blue frees his top (left) leg, White posts his left hand in front of himself instead of keeping hold of Blue. Blue takes what White gives him and gains an opportunity to take his back.

White begins to under-hook Blue's leg.

Blue's left palm is under White's right elbow.

Blue quickly comes up onto his bottom (right) elbow…

…and throws his left arm over White's back to keep White from posturing. Note that his right elbow is no longer under White.

Blue post his right hand as he takes White's back.

Blue's top leg drives White's head toward the mat. Blue turns his entire body as he pushes White's elbow up.

Blue frees his left knee at the same time as he pushes White's right elbow.

Blue briefly puts his left foot in White's hip to stop White from coming forward while Blue transitions.

Blue posts his right palm off to his right and pulls himself on top with his other arm.

Blue puts in his hook and solidifies his position.

Here, Blue has under-hooked one of White's arms. If he wanted to flatten White out, he would under-hook both arms and then extend his body, driving White forward.

❷ Blue has multiple options if he can push White's elbow from behind. Here, White is farther around Blue's side, and his hips are not as free to move backwards.

▲ Blue does not have the angle he needs, so he lets go of the elbow and pushes White's side so that he can free his hips.

The best time for Blue to attempt the sweep is when he feels White trying to lift up his chest or remove his tangled arm.

Blue takes his top leg off White's shoulder, intending to hook his foot in White's far (left) leg.

In this situation, White's left hand will typically be holding Blue's bottom leg or, as shown, posting on the mat. Either way, White's arm will get trapped, at least for a moment or two.

Blue sits up on his elbow right away and reaches across White for his belt at his side. Blue holds White near his elbow.

As White goes over, Blue keeps his leg tight to White and uses his hook to help pull himself over White. Blue pushes off the mat with his free foot, and White's momentum helps Blue end on top.

◉ This time, White is just about all the way around to Blue's side. Blue again attacks White's elbow as he tries to pass.

White begins to reach for the lapel grip.

Blue puts his left palm under White's right elbow as White reaches for Blue's lapel.

White does not let go as Blue pushes his elbow.

Blue prevents White's arm from coming forward with his bottom (right) hand. Blue could also grab White's wrist from the beginning.

White's right arm is being torqued, and he has to lean forward to relieve the pressure.

As White drops forward, Blue comes up on his knees.

Raising the hips is the final touch. White gets rolled.

Blue transitions into side control.

Blue pushes on White's elbow and at the same time goes to his knees.

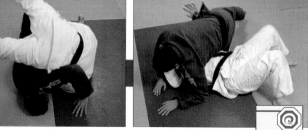

Blue lets go with his left hand but keeps the grip with the right until White goes over. This stops White from fixing his base.

⊙ Some moves do not get much use because it is easy to see them coming. This is one of those moves. A novice guard passer will fall for this one. Once he has he probably will not repeat the mistake. Even so, the move comes in handy against advanced players, because once you establish the grip, the opponent is forced to try something else.

White tries to pass by under-hooking both legs and stacking Blue.

Blue knows what is coming, so he grabs White's collar fingers in, thumbs facing down.

As White lifts, Blue pulls down with his arms and lifts his legs.

White puts himself into the trap by trying to lift up in his effort to stack Blue.

Blue turns his wrists into White's carotids. His legs come to the top of White's shoulders.

Blue crosses his ankles and then straightens his legs. As he does he pushes his thighs into his forearms, adding power to his arms. Blue straightens his fists, driving the knuckles into White's carotids.

⊙ As with many chokes, the key is to take out all the slack and then use large muscle groups for power to finish the move.

◉ Sometimes, in order to pull an opponent in tight, you first need to make space. This technique is such an example. White breaks Blue's legs open and brings his knee in. White wants to be tight once his knee comes through. Blue cannot push White back, but he can slide himself away. Once that happens, Blue has space to close his guard.

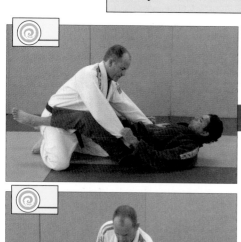

Blue's legs are open.

White tries to pass by bringing his knee between Blue's legs.

Blue pushes White's knee. He does so to make himself slide back and stop White from following.

Once he has created space, Blue can put his feet in White's hips.

Blue holds White's sleeves to keep White from grabbing his legs.

With White extended, it is easy for Blue to pull his arms forward and replace the guard.

White is trying to under-hook Blue's right leg.

As soon as White starts to reach for the under-hook, Blue turns to that same side and grabs White's wrist.

Blue snakes his butt back. He pushes off his feet for help and places his left foot in White's hip.

That makes space for Blue to bring his leg across White's body.

Blue hooks his foot around White's left hip.

To finish the submission, Blue pins White's hand against his hip, straightens his leg, and, for the final power, turns his torso. The submission works the shoulder, or possibly the elbow.

The foot needs to come all the way across and hook the waist.

Guard Pass Counters: Smash Pass Defenses

single under-hook

Early defense: Come up on one elbow and pull down on their head with your other hand. Hook under their leg and grab their wrist.

On-time defense: Push with both hands against their shoulders. Use straight arms to get your knee in their chest, then push them away with that knee and fix your guard.

Late defense, snake move: Straight-arm their chest before they come down. Post your free leg and use it to pull your hips away and make space. Replace your bottom leg first.

Late defense, push the elbow: Before they drop all the way, push the inside of their under-hooking elbow with the palm of your hand. Turn on your side for space, and bring your top knee behind their armpit.

Armbar: After your knee is out, lean back. If they do not let go of their collar grip, their arm will straighten, giving you an armbar. Squeeze your knees as you drive their shoulder down and extend their elbow.

Armbar follow-up: Continue driving their shoulder down. Without losing contact with your top knee, circle your shin in front of their face, then push their head away as you push your hips into their elbow.

Take the back: If they post on the arm you are attacking, quickly come up on your elbow. Reach around their back with your other hand, then go from elbow to palm with the first hand. Pull yourself ontop and put in the hooks.

Sweep: You push off their elbow but cannot get your knee free: With your chest against their back, hook behind their top knee with your top foot. Pull back with your arm, lean back, and lift with your hook.

Roll the elbow: If they do not let go of your collar when you push up on their elbow, their arm tweaks at the elbow. Push their elbow to the mat. Drive your hips back into theirs as you go to your knees.

double under-hook

Double under-hook defense: Hold their collars with both hands, fingers in. As they lift, drive your index finger knuckles into their neck as the pinky-side of your hands tightens their collar. Cross your feet and straighten your legs.

CHAPTER 3

CHOKES

Here, we begin to look at techniques for attacking from the guard. Chokes are a good place to start, because even when they do not work, the attempts open up other opportunities. The collar grips used for chokes present a problem that must be dealt with before the guard can be passed. Once you have a good lapel grip, opportunities for armlocks and sweeps will present themselves, especially as your opponent defends against a choke.

Most of the chokes shown could be classified as low risk maneuvers. Attempting them is not likely to lead to a worse position for the guard player if they fail. That is in contrast to the basic arm lock (juji-gatame) or the triangle (sangaku-jime), both of which, when they do not work, put you in greater danger of having your guard passed.

At first glance, chokes appear primarily to involve the hands and forearms. The hands and forearms are indeed crucial elements, but core body movement is vital once again. Pay close attention to the movement of the torso in each of the examples. There is much more power in your torso than in your hands and forearms. The strength of your torso is used to amplify the power of the limbs.

WARNING: The chokes shown here are meant to work by squeezing the carotid arteries on the sides of the neck. Restriction of blood flow makes the chokes work, not a deprivation of air. Chokes that block the windpipe are very dangerous and can cause death by collapsing the windpipe. Sometimes it is enough to block just one of the carotid arteries to make your opponent tap, but typically you must block both. Sometimes a "choke" puts enough pressure on your opponent's face or jaw that he submits. That sort of "choke" is not very sporting and tends to cause the teeth to cut up the inside of the mouth. Obviously, it is rude to do that sort of thing to your training partners.

Given that chokes work by closing off the carotid arteries, special attention should be paid to concentrating force on them. The best way to apply acute pressure to the arteries is with either edge of the wrist or the bones on either edge of the hand. The angle of the choke should roughly follow your opponent's jaw-line. In other words, it should not be at a right angle to his spine; it should slant upward from the front of the throat to the back of the neck.

Always warm up before practicing submission techniques. This is particularly important if you are on the receiving end of a choke, it literally being your neck. Be cautious of your partner's safety. It is everyone's responsibility to tap out before they pass out or get hurt. The reality though, is that sometimes people pass out before they tap, so be cautious and let go immediately if it happens.

⌾ **Bones make chokes.** The highlighted areas are the most effective parts of the arms for pushing into the carotid arteries.

◉ The **X**-choke is considered a basic move. However, do not confuse *basic* with *easy to master*, or *simple to defeat*.

▲ ▼ ▽ The hands must reach deep into the lapels. Use the edges of the hands/wrists so that the bones push into the neck.

▲ ▼ ▽ The thumbs are out; the fingers do the work. The thumb bones or edges of the wrists are what make the pressure on the carotid arteries.

▲ ▼ ▽ Blue curls his wrists back. As he does, he turns his wrists as if he were cracking a whip. The action is vital for putting acute pressure on White's arteries.

▲ ▼ ▽ Blue pulls his wrists back toward his chest and crunches forward.

▲ ▶ ▶ ▶ Notice how Blue uses his torso. First, he moves to his left, and that helps him get a deep grip.

As he moves even farther to the left, Blue levers up White's head with his forearm.

Blue reaches across with his left hand and grabs in deeply with his four fingers.

When Blue twists back, his torso movement powers the choke.

Blue pulls White to his chest. His elbows are tight to his sides. Blue's head is up as his hands come down.

❷ This time, White tries to fight off the *X*-choke by pushing away and bringing up his head.

White postures. Instead of trying to muscle White back down, Blue reverses direction with White. Blue turns his wrists in the direction opposite the *X*-choke and grinds the knuckles of his pinky and ring fingers into White's carotids. In other words, he turns his palms down. This pulls White's collar tighter and forces Blue's knuckles into White's carotid arteries. It may also work if Blue can make pressure with the blade of his hand, but he must use the bony edge.

Instead of pulling in his elbows, this is a thrusting motion. As in the *X*-choke, Blue's wrists are touching each other.

 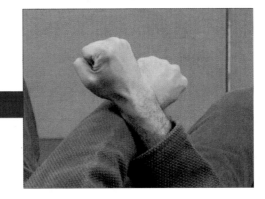

⊚ If your opponent takes a defensive posture, with his head to your chest, he puts his neck and the collar around it, within reach. In this technique, White's head is off-center to the side he is facing. We will cover what to do if his head is off-center to the other side in the next spread.

Both the sequences on this spread finish the same way, with an **X**-choke. But the entries are a little different.

White is controlling Blue's hips but is not trying to advance his position.

Blue takes the initiative and pushes White's head.

With his grips in place, Blue snakes his hips out and comes partially to his side.

With a deep right grip established, Blue levers up White's head to make space for a deep left grip.

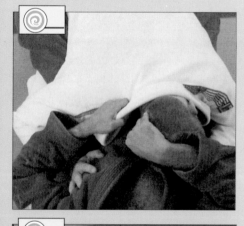

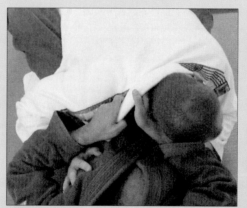

This time, Blue pulls White's head with his right hand. He pulls open White's collar as he does.

Quickly, he reaches four fingers in with his right hand as he continues to hold open White's collar with his left hand.

Blue lifts White's head with his right forearm and makes space for his left grip. The second hand goes under the first arm.

Blue wedges in his right forearm so that White cannot bring his head back.

Blue uses his left hand to pull White's lapel, making space for him to grab the lapel with his right hand.

Blue uses his right grip for leverage to work his forearm under White's head.

Blue reaches palms up, four fingers in, and deep.

Blue twists back, sinking in the choke as he does.

Note that Blue goes from his back to his side and to his back again.

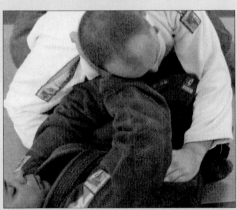

❷ Here is a counter to a common and effective **X**-choke defense. We put it here because the players are in a positions very similar to the last technique. However, this defense is employed against the **X**-choke generally, so look for the counter anytime you see the defense. The essence of this counter is that Blue works around the defense by causing White's forearm to press against his own carotid artery.

Blue attempts an **X**-choke.

White defends by swimming his right arm between Blue's arms and sliding his palm back...

...across the side of his head to help wedge his forearm between Blue's forearm and his own neck.

White has to move his head off-center to make space to put in his arm. That is the opening Blue wants.

▶▶▶ Blue demonstrates how his body moves during the technique. He gets to his side, locks his feet, and crunches his head toward his knees.

Blue goes with the flow. As White swims his arm through, Blue turns to his side.

Blue's turn undermines White's base, which allows Blue to move to White's side.

From his sideways position, Blue crosses his ankles, squeezes with his legs, and crunches with his torso.

The bottom (left) hand is the power hand. The other hand helps choke White with his own arm.

From his side, Blue makes pressure into White's defending right hand, choking White with White's own right arm.

⊙ Once again, White is in a very defensive posture, and once again White is looking to his left. But unlike in the previous technique, this time White's head is off-center to Blue's other side, so that he is looking across Blue's center line. Blue does not have a good angle for levering up White's head with his right arm this time. Instead, he will work in the choke from the front of White's head.

Blue uses his thumb to hook White's collar and fish it out, but the power of his grip will come from his fingers.

Blue's left hand grips directly behind White's spine.

Blue forces his knuckles along White's jaw line, starting near White's ear and working his way across the neck. He snakes his hips out just a bit as he does.

Crude but effective, White's head is turned, and Blue finds space to reach his arm across to the lapel. Note how Blue rotates his torso to help him get his grip.

 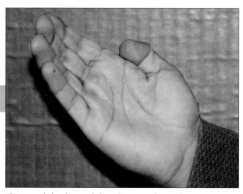

To get his hand under White's chin, Blue points his knuckles as shown. If he made a complete fist, it would require too much space to get his hand through.

Once his hand is through, Blue opens his fingers and feels for the lapel grip.

Blue rotates off to the side to make it possible for him to bring his forearm over White's head.

Blue needs to move his left forearm over to the other side of White's head quickly.

Once his forearm clears White's head, Blue drops his elbow and moves his center line back into alignment with White's.

A solid grip is needed, but the power comes from the body, not the hands.

◉ This grip is the same as in the previous technique but here the entry and execution are similar to the **X**-choke. From the angle of attack pictured, four-fingers-in with both hands is a better grip, all things being equal. But all things are not equal, and sometimes a thumb-in grip is the only option, or at least the better one.

▲ ▼The photos above illustrate the position of Blue's hands, and the ones below show the actual choke. As the choke is applied, the action of each wrist drives into White's neck, applying pressure to the neck from both directions. Blue flexes his right wrist in the direction of his thumb and the left in the direction of his pinky finger. The action of the wrists is the finishing touch, and hence should come at the finish of the move.

◉ Blue could also make a choke with both hands thumbs in. That would not be an ideal grip, but again, situations may arise where it is the only option. Even when both thumbs are in, the power of the grip is from the fingers. The thumbs help get the hands in place while the gripping is done with the fingers.

Here, the grip starts the same as on the previous page but finishes differently. This is very similar to the technique on pg. 55.

Blue opens White's lapel to make it easier to get his initial collar grip.

Blue turns slightly to his side so he can reach deeper.

The left-hand grip also helps to prevent White from sitting up as a defense against the deep-collar grip.

Blue begins to move his head to the other side.

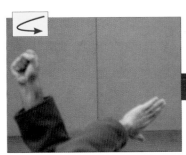   

Blue pulls White down and himself up as he moves his head to the other side.

Blue grips thumb first with his other hand.

White resists. Blue senses he will be able to make the modified *X*-choke work and changes tactics.

Blue twists his right hand palm down and pushes the pinky side edge into White's neck.

By turning to his side, Blue makes good angles for his hands to enter. By turning back, he generates power through his torso.

To finish the choke, Blue twists his right hand counter-clockwise; that has the effect of twisting the lapel more tightly around White's neck and of digging the pinky side edge of his wrist into White's carotid artery. Blue can only tighten the collar this way about an inch, so it is vital that things are tight before he starts.

⊙ If you can use your legs against your opponent's head to add to the pressure of the choke, you can add a lot of power and range of motion to your attack.

Blue is attempting an **X**-choke.

As he moves his hips, he gives White a chance to bring his arm through, perhaps for a smash pass.

As White reaches through, and before he can establish position and weight on Blue's leg, Blue makes his counter.

Blue uses his right leg to snake his hips out to the side and a little bit away from White. The hip movement is crucial.

Blue takes his shin over White's head and then brings it under his chin.

Blue snakes his hips a little bit to the right to improve his angle of attack. He finishes by pushing his leg into White's neck and pulling with his arms at the same time.

Use this technique when your opponent counters the **X**-Choke by putting his fist in your neck.

Blue sets up an **X**-choke. First, he comes up and to the left, reaching deep inside White's lapel.

Blue moves back, reaches under his first (right) arm with his second (left) hand and gets his grip, four fingers in on both sides.

White counters by grabbing Blue's lapel and posting into his fist, which is in Blue's neck. Blue makes pressure on his own neck if he pulls.

Instead, Blue puts his foot down and snakes to the same side as White's stiff arm. This makes space for him to put his left foot in White's hip.

Blue puts his foot in White's hip and pushes off. Note how his upper body moves back.

Now that White is outstretched, he can no longer make pressure. At this point, White is worried about his base.

Now Blue can sit up and sink in the choke. Once he does, White can no longer stiff-arm for defense.

Blue crunches forward and completes the choke.

Blue takes a high collar grip with his right hand, four fingers in.

Blue pulls himself up with the collar grip.

Blue needs to come up high enough to wrap his left arm around White's head and grab his own sleeve.

Blue uses his thumb to help get the grip for his fingers.

The thumb holds the sleeve, but the strength of the grip is from the fingers.

Once the grip is secure, the left elbow drives down and the right elbow comes up.

Blue slides his thumb into the end of his sleeve and uses it to gather up the cloth for his fingers.

Blue grips his sleeve with four fingers to the outside. He can relax his thumb at this point.

To finish the choke, Blue drops his left elbow, pulls on his right sleeve, and lifts his right elbow. As usual, he is careful to turn the bony parts of his hands/wrists into White's neck. In this case, it is the thumb side of both wrists (see pg. 55).

If need be, Blue will use his right leg to hold down White's left leg so that White cannot turn with the choke. If White manages to turn with the choke, Blue has an easy opportunity to scissors sweep White to Blue's left.

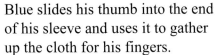 Look for the sleeve choke if your opponent drops his head while you have a lapel grip. If his posture is good and his head is up, you will not be able to get your second arm far enough around the back of his head to grip your sleeve end properly.

Blue already has his deep collar grip. He snakes his hips left and as he moves his head right.

Once his head is off to the side, he takes his second grip, thumb in.

White immediately defends by grabbing Blue's lapel and thrusting his fist in Blue's neck.

Blue counters by moving his hips out and bringing his leg over.

Blue puts his leg on the side of White's head.

Blue pushes away with his legs and turns his fists as pictured below.

▲ ▶ ▶ ▶ This is the hand action Blue uses above. Two things happen as he turns his hands from the third picture to the fourth. First, the lapel is cinched more tightly behind White's neck. Second, Blue's right hand switches from thumb-side to pinky-side against White's neck . That rotation makes pressure on White's carotid artery.

If the choke does not work, the armbar is right there. Blue wants his leg wrapped high over White's head for the armbar.

Blue lets go of his thumb-in grip and uses that arm to pin White's arm to his chest.

Blue uses both his arms to hold White's arm. Blue forces White down with his legs as he raises his hips. Blue pinches his knees together.

Chokes: X-Choke, Standard Grip

◎ *Make pressure to the carotid arteries with the bones in your hands and wrists, and with the lapels.*
◎ *Change angles and techniques to counter defenses.*

▶ Vs. basic posture: Four fingers in, grab deeply and angle your arms under the jaw-line. Change the angle of your upper body back and forth for better angles and power.

▶ Keep your elbows close to your sides as you sit up. Curl back the wrists and protrude the wrists into their carotid arteries

▶ They posture up: Reverse the position of the hands and straighten the arms, tightening the lapel grip and digging into the carotids with the pinky-side edges of the hands.

▶ Head in your chest, looking away: Feed the collar to the other hand, four fingers in. Lever up their head, and turn your upper body. Set in the X-choke, and turn back your torso for increased choking power.

▶ Head in your chest, looking across: Take a thumb-in grip on the lapel from over the top. Grind your hand in under their jaw-line. Turn to the side to create an angle to drop your forearm to the side of their head. Twist back to finish.

  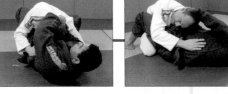 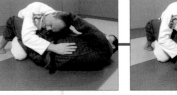 

▶ When you drive your hand in, keep your bottom knuckles almost straight while curling the middle and top. Once your hand is across the throat, open the hand and grab the lapel.

▶ They defend with an arm: Choke them with their own arm. Get way off to the side and focus power through your arm into his. Use your core muscles to crunch as you tighten.

▶ They straight arm your throat: Put your feet in their hips, push your hips away, and sit up. Keep them away with your feet on their hips, and re-apply the X-choke.

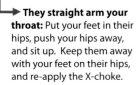    

Chokes: X-Choke, Thumb-In Grip

- ***The thumb-in grip is not as strong as the four-fingers-in, but it is easier to obtain and opens up some nice follow-ups.***
- ***Use the thumb to set up the grip, but make the fingers to do the work.***

[repeated from last page]
Their head in your chest, looking across: Take a thumb-in grip on the lapel from over the top. Grind your hand in under his jaw-line. Turn to the side to create an angle to drop your forearm to the side of his head. Twist back to finish.

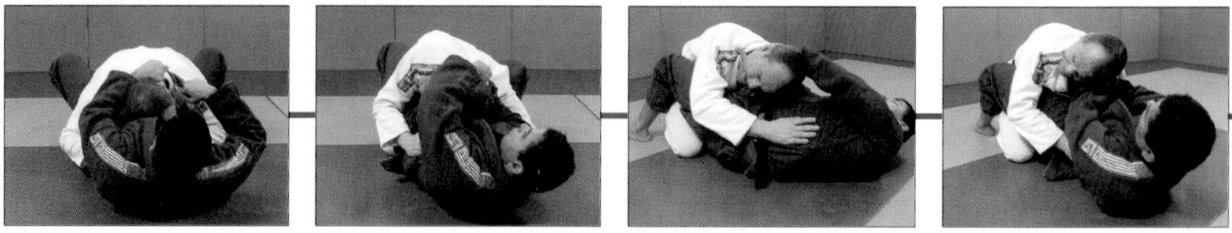

They scoop your leg: Use your shin to push into their jaw-line as you pull tight your *X*-choke.

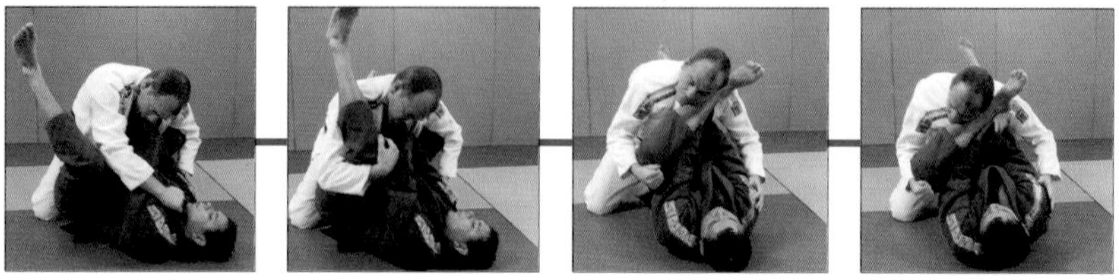

They straight arm your throat vs. thumb-in grip: Put your legs in an armbar position. The hand with the four-fingers-in grip twists palm down and thrusts. Push with the legs.

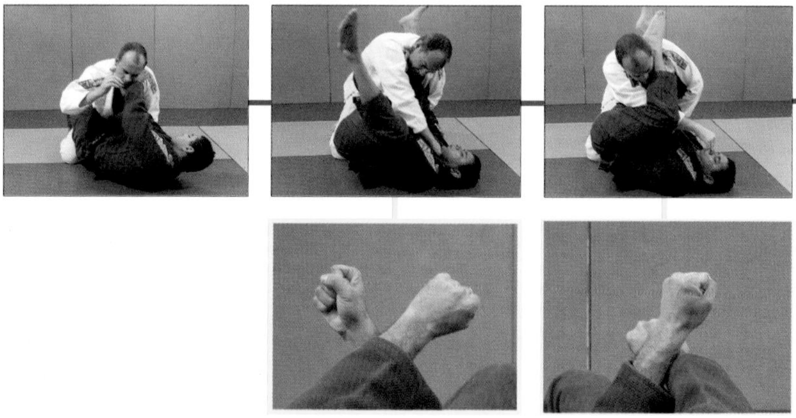

Switch to armbar: If the chokes are not working, switch to something else. White is giving his arm, so Blue takes it.

Chokes: Sleeve Wheel

▶ **They sit up:** You sit up too. Take a four-fingers-in grip and lift that elbow high. Grab the end of your own sleeve with the other hand. One elbow goes up; the other pulls down.

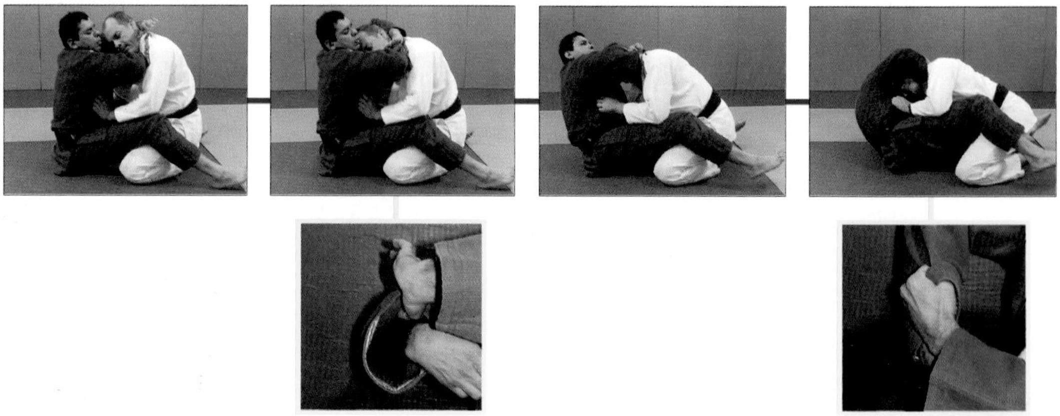

CHAPTER 4

SWEEPS

The guard is a good place from which to attempt submissions. But the mount and side control are better and are also vastly superior places from which to throw strikes. It is almost always in your interest to improve your position unless improving position would be at the expense of a solid opportunity for a submission. From the guard, there are basically three options for improving one's position: sweeps, taking the back, and standing up. Here, we look at sweeps, and, in particular, sweeps against a kneeling opponent.

With the exception of the *T*-sweep at the end of the chapter, all of the techniques in this chapter are based on the *scissors sweep*. All of the sweeps, rely on controlling one or both of the opponent's arm and then making him fall over that shoulder. Anytime you have control of one of your opponent's arms from the guard, consider whether you can force him over that shoulder. If you can do so while still controlling that arm, he will be swept.

As you look through the techniques in this chapter, note how one attack leads to another. Such is the nature of jiu-jitsu.

A key point to bear in mind with the scissors sweep, and most others, is that it will be easier if your torso is off center from your opponent's (see the illustrations below). That is to say that you do not want your opponent's head and spine lined up with your own. If you want to sweep to your left, the opponent should be to your left as the move begins. The way to accomplish this positioning is by first snaking out your butt. Hip and torso movement, as usual, are key.

Conversely, the easiest way for the top player to stuff the sweep is to keep repositioning himself so that he is centered over the guard player.

It can be very difficult to sweep an opponent who is substantially larger than you. If you find yourself in such a situation, consider focusing on submissions or taking the back. Whatever the case may be, do not be so determined to sweep that you give up a chance for something better.

❷ This is a good example of an attack using a sleeve-and-lapel grip. The sleeve-and-lapel grip makes a good starting point for attacking from the bottom, because it can be used for sweeps, chokes, or armlocks.

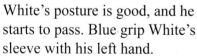

White's posture is good, and he starts to pass. Blue grip White's sleeve with his left hand.

White lifts his leg to make space for his arm or to help open Blue's legs. Before White can progress, Blue grabs the lapel four fingers in. Without letting go of the grip, Blue turns the palm of his hand toward White's chest.

Blue straightens his arm into White's chest to stop him from smashing into Blue. At the same time, he turns to his side. Blue positions his left leg low to the mat and against White's knee. His right knee slides across, and his foot hooks White's hip.

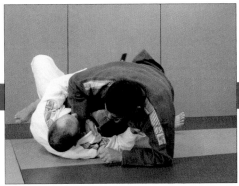

It is important that Blue snake his hips out somewhat. Blue needs to be off to the side a bit, not straight under White. Blue scissors his legs, yanks with his left arm, and continues the turn to his side. Blue pulls White's arm like he would pull the cord to start a gas lawn mower.

Blue follows through. Once White is over, Blue is free to use his left arm to help bring himself up into the mount. Once White is on his back, Blue can switch from pushing White with his right foot to acting as an anchor with which Blue can pull himself over.

Blue keeps the lapel grip. Since his forearm is already across White's throat, Blue has ended in a good place to follow up with a choke.

☯ It goes without saying that things do not always go as planned. Blue attempts the scissors sweep, but White keeps his balance and counters with an attempt to pass. Blue goes to plan *B*.

Blue starts with a sleeve-and-lapel grip.

As Blue attempts his sweep, White counters with good base.

Because of all the space that has been created between the two, Blue needs to sit up and into White.

Blue comes up onto his elbow.

White goes on the offensive, swimming his arm under Blue's leg.

Blue must change tactics. Blue shifts his body away from White. He does so both with hip movement and by simply pushing off with his right arm and leg.

Blue switches the position of his left leg so that his foot is on White's knee. Blue starts to turn back the other way and hooks his right foot under White's knee.

Blue sits up and then right away twists to his left. He pushes with the lower leg and lifts with the higher. Blue pulls on White's left arm at the same time.

Blue's arm levers White's head up. The action of Blue's left arm is not just to pull White's arm. He also repositions his elbow to help him transition to the top.

Blue switches to palm on the mat so that he can quickly move into a solid mounted position.

White lifts his leg, and his upper body is upright. Blue attacks with the scissors sweep.

White feels what is happening and drops both his leg and his upper body. At this point, the scissors sweep will not work.

In order for this sweep to work, Blue needs both of White's arms to one side.

Blue pulls the belt as he drops his left shoulder to the mat and twists to his right. As he does he traces an arc with his right knee and lifts White.

Note that Blue is still holding White's elbow.

White's momentum helps Blue to end on top. Blue pulls on White's elbow to help turn himself.

❷ An easy way for White to stuff the scissors sweep is by lowering his butt and upper body on the outside of Blue's top knee. Doing so not only lowers White's center of gravity, but it also tends to immobilize Blue's top leg. Here is a counter for that scenario.

Another technique for getting both of the opponent's arms to one side appears on the next spread.

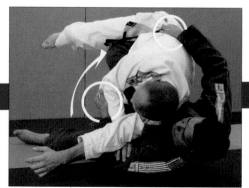

Blue pushes over White's arm. The twisting motion of his upper body helps Blue make power to move White's arm and upsets his base.

Blue comes up on his left elbow. His chest must come up to the back of White's shoulder. This gives Blue control of White's arm and prevents White from pulling it out.

Blue reaches over White's back with his top arm. He grabs White's belt at the outside of his hip. The moment to sweep is when White tries to rise and free his left arm.

Blue immediately steps his left leg over.

Blue hooks his left foot under White's right knee and fixes his position.

Blue's chest remains pressed to White's shoulder the whole time. White is in a tough spot.

Blue starts the scissors sweep, but White prevents the move by dropping his upper body and holding with his left arm.

Blue recognizes the sweep will not work and turns his attention to underhooking White's left arm. Blue keeps a firm grip on White's right elbow.

Blue brings his right shoulder toward his own ear so that it is easier for his hand to under-hook. Blue gets maximum leverage by threading his arm under and inside White's elbow.

White is now concerned about the sweep from the previous spread, so he does not push his left side back towards Blue.

Blue's response is to go back to a variation on the scissors sweep.

White gets rolled because his elbow is trapped and he cannot base out with his right arm.

▲ ▼ This is a good point to segue into the attack series starting on pg. 112.

Blue scoops up and under. Blue uses his right shin to push into White's hip, giving him space to thread under his right arm better.

Blue's biceps pushes White's arm at the inside of White's elbow. Blue brings White's left arm in front of Blue's chest.

Blue comes up on his elbow. It is crucial that Blue's chest is tight to White's left shoulder so that White cannot pull his left arm free.

Blue's left leg is blocking White's right knee and Blue's left hand controls White's elbow as Blue's right leg powers White to his back.

Blue uses his right arm and leg for purchase to pull himself on top.

Blue ends in the mount. He keeps his chest tight to the back of White's arm, ready to follow up.

Scissors Sweeps

◉ *Use all of your limbs and get to your side when you sweep your opponent.*

◉ *Be prepared to counter your opponent's defenses.*

Look for the basic scissors sweep when they are on one or both knees and their shoulders are high: Be decisive. Get to your side. Push with the top hand and pull with the bottom hand. The top leg pushes in coordination with the top hand as the bottom leg reaps the opponent's knee.

If your opponent under hooks your top leg: Turn partly back from your side and hook your instep under their knee. Come up on your elbow, sit forward, lift with your instep. Your bottom leg blocks their other knee.

If they drop their upper body to stuff the scissors sweep: Push their arm across holding near the elbow, or scoop under it and bring it in front of you that way. Bring your chest tight to the back of their arm, like for an arm-drag. Grab across and hold their belt at the far side of their hips. Pull on their belt, lean back, and lift with your top knee in one coordinated motion.

If they drop their upper body to stuff the scissors sweep: If they stop the sweep above by moving away from you after you get to the arm-drag position, sweep them away from you. You must have control of their far elbow (White's right). Get up on your elbow. Make the scissors action with your legs as in the first technique and stay close as they roll over so that you end on top in the mount.

CHAPTER 5

ARMBARS

The straight armbar (juji-gatame) from the bottom is perhaps the quintessential guard attack. The flip side is that most players have at least some idea how to defend it. The most common defense is to smash back into the guard player so that he cannot extend his torso to straighten out the arm. This sort of defense allows the top player to put his own weight and gravity on his side. Time is on the guard passer's side once he stacks his opponent.

Once you have been stacked, it can be very difficult to maneuver or straighten out for the finish. Powering back into a smashing defense from the guard is an option; your torso is a strong group of muscles. However, you can damage your lower back this way, and if you do, it might never be the same.

Even if your back is strong, sometimes powering the submission just doesn't work. The better practice is to deflect force and try to use it to your advantage.

In this chapter, we look at the basic armlock and then examine a number of options against stacking and other defenses. With all of the techniques, it is best to go before your opponent can bear down on you solidly and establish stability. The further he compresses you, the worse things tend to become. Take your opportunities when they arise. Learning to recognize them is an objective of practice. After you have practiced the moves shown in isolation, have your partner apply his weight in the different directions discussed and see if you can make the appropriate counter based upon feeling his weight.

Key Points:

○ **Thumb up:** Apply the submission in the direction opposite of where your opponent's thumb would be pointing if he had it sticking out like a hitch-hiker. Turn the opponent's thumb where you want it to be. Use both arms to control your opponent's forearm when possible.

○ **Knees together:** Your knees squeeze together. This constricts your opponent's arm, giving it less room to move, and hence less chance for him to escape. Your knees aren't exactly trying to touch each other, however, because sometimes your hips need to be tilted and bringing the knees precisely together would mean squaring them.

Pull at an angle: Don't use your privates as a fulcrum. Pull off to one side and/or into the side of your leg. Pay attention to the direction of the thumb as you do.

○ **Leverage:** You have more leverage to straighten the arm the closer to the wrist you hold. Sometimes it is necessary to grab at the elbow while you put your legs in position, but as you try to straighten the arm, work your hold away from the elbow.

○ **Control the head:** The leg that goes over your opponent's head controls it. Keep pressure on your opponent's head with that leg.

○ **Leg goes high:** Bring the leg that does not go over your opponent's head go high up his back. Try to bring the lower leg all the way to your opponent's armpit.

White has good base, his arms are not straight, and his weight is on his elbows. ▲ In the top example, Blue starts by controlling White's elbow with his left hand; ▲ in the bottom, he holds with his right hand.

Blue's right hand comes over the top of White's arm, and he holds at the elbow. Note the grip Blue uses: his thumb is next to his fingers--the monkey grip.

Blue snakes to the side, holding White's elbow in place while Blue's moves his hips under. His left hand holds over White's collar bone. Blue's forearm is pressed against White's face.

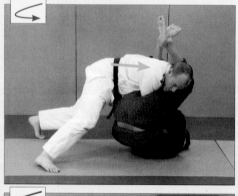

Blue needs to feel the way White is directing his weight and use that force to his advantage.

White is powering forward, so Blue pushes the same way and up. Most of Blue's power goes through the back of the leg that is across White's chest.

Blue's other leg directs White's head. Blue is rolling White over the shoulder of his trapped arm.

Blue's hand position prevents White from moving backward. His forearm position prevents White from smashing down to defend. His arms help him turn perpendicular to White.

Blue's right leg is high up White's back as his other leg comes over White's head. Blue will squeeze his knees together as he thrusts forward his hips. If Blue extends White's arm, White will have to tap.

White smashes into Blue to prevent his arm from being extended.

White is a table with a missing leg.

During the sweep, Blue has switched grips with his right hand. This keeps White tighter and limits the chance of escape. This is not strictly necessary but is advisable.

Blue uses both his arms on White's one arm for the finish. Blue has White's thumb up and pulls in the opposite direction, knees tight.

White stacks Blue to prevent the armbar. **This time, he drives his head in the direction of Blue's head.** This is better technique on White's part.

Blue must use his left arm to control White's right arm. He needs his right arm to help him pivot.

Blue's right hand comes out from under to push on White's leg. Blue does not let himself get stacked on his neck. He pivots on his upper back. Blue's head remains free and travels in a semi-circle under White.

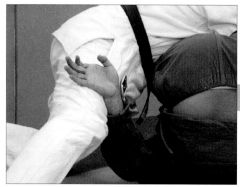

To get his spin started, Blue can hook White's leg with the back of his hand if he has far to reach.

❷ From any given position, there are a number of options for both players. If you have an answer for whatever the opponent tries ready to go when the moment presents itself, opportunity is on your side.

Whichever way White tries to smash Blue, Blue has a method for redirecting White's counter.

▶▶▶ White is closer here, so Blue hooks his hand in a conventional manner, palm to White's leg.

Blue's right arm helps him extend his upper body.

Once his upper body straightens out, Blue will turn to his shoulder, extend, and then turn belly-down.

Blue curls the leg around White's head for control and to take range of motion away from White. Blue finishes the armlock belly-down.

As Blue's upper body comes through, his hand rotates as well.

As he goes belly-down to finish the submission, he uses both hands to control White's arm.

White defends, and Blue is not able to finish the armbar. Usually this is because the top player grabs his other hand or some material to help keep his arm bent.

In his efforts to save his arm, White commits most of his weight to his upper body. This makes it possible for Blue to lift White's lower body without much effort.

Blue grabs White's ankle. He could have grabbed White's pants instead, but the ankle provides more control.

Blue lifts and pulls on White's ankle. At the same time, Blue rolls to his back. The rotation of his body is the source of power.

Blue crosses both of his arms over White's arm. Blue's left foot is hooked around White's shoulder, and his feet are close to each other. That takes away more space from White.

Blue's keeps his legs tight as he hugs White's arm, leans back, and raises his hips to finish the armbar.

❂ If you can avoid being stacked/smashed, you have better chances to finish the armbar, and the same is true for the triangle. But sometimes it happens. The techniques in this chapter are counters to stacking defenses. But even with these techniques at your disposal, you are better off making your move before your opponent can settle into base and smash into you, so don't wait...go, keep moving. Also, expect your opponent to try to fix his base, and as he does, gauge the direction of his pressure and switch techniques accordingly.

This time, when Blue attempts the armbar, **White smashes in the direction of Blue's right side.**

Blue gets into position for the armbar, but White is able to keep his arm bent and smash back down into Blue. The direction to which White smashes is the direction to which Blue pushes White. Here, that is in the direction Blue's knees are pointing.

Blue lifts his hips and plants his hand on the mat. Pushing off the planted hand helps Blue rotate his head free.

Blue rolls back over his right shoulder, **not** over his neck. His left hand helps him push into White and makes it easier for Blue to roll over his right shoulder.

Blue brings his head through as White is pushed the other way.

Blue adjusts the position of his hand to make things easier on himself.

Blue applies the armbar, belly-down by thrusting his hips forward, keeping his knees tight, and straightening White's right arm opposite the direction of his thumb.

Blue's legs curl, and he lifts his feet toward the ceiling. This keeps the armbar tight and helps prevent White from spinning out to escape.

Instead of lifting his upper body, White tries to get a grip behind Blue's neck and smash.

Blue braces his leg with his arm so that White cannot smash it down.

Blue positions the side of his right wrist just above White's elbow. He hold his hands together, palm to palm. His fingers are not laced.

> ❂ In the previous techniques, Blue never let go of the armbar and finished with it. Sometimes a better strategy is to switch the point of attack. You might attack one arm with the intent of going for the other, or you might just end up attacking the other if your opponent defends.

If White's hand is on the wrong side of Blue's head ▲, or if he turns his elbow free ▲, Blue follows up with the *omo-plata*.

Blue uses one hand (the left) to control White's arm, and the grasps White's belt with the other.

Blue straightens out his legs and pulls himself up. He pivots on his butt as he does. Blue must hold White's back so White does not roll out of the technique.

Blue grinds his wrist into the bottom of White's triceps. Blue brings his shoulder and ear together so that they squeeze White's arm, making it difficult for White to rotate his elbow as a defense.

Blue pushes with his legs to extend White's arm by pushing himself one way and White's upper body the other.

❷ If White were to escape the elbow lock by rotating his palm up at this point, Blue would immediately transition to the omo plata technique below.

Blue goes from his elbow to his palm. He is now parallel to White. His legs shoot straight forward, driving White's shoulder to the mat.

Blue bases on his palm and scoots his butt away from White. Blue's knees switch also. Blue wants to keep White's shoulder planted on the mat.

Blue leans forward and lifts his butt to finish the submission. Blue's upper body position prevents White from rolling.

❷ One technique leads to another. Your opponent will give you something; recognizing it and knowing what to do with it are half the battle. In this particular case, when White steps near Blue's head, he makes space for Blue to attack White's leg.

Blue attempts an armbar but White pulls his arm out and clears his elbow above Blue's hips, thus eliminating the danger.

White plants his foot towards Blue's head for better base. This gives Blue space he can use.

Blue scoops up White's leg. Blue drops his knee down and between White's legs. He makes pressure with the inside of his knee and at the same time keeps his foot firmly against White's side.

Blue pulls White's leg with his arm and pushes away with his knee, bracing his back off the mat.

The danger of kneebars is that damage occurs to the opponent before it really starts to hurt. That makes it easy for your training partners to hurt themselves without realizing it. Both players need to recognize and be aware of this danger.

Blue's other leg wraps around White's hamstrings.

Now the foot pushes the back of White's leg. Blue switches from holding at White's knee to holding closer to the ankle.

Blue controls both of White's legs, one with his hands and one with his feet.

Blue triangles his legs while maintaining control of both of White's legs. Blue squeezes his knees, lifts his hips, and keeps his elbows tight to finish the kneebar.

The mechanics of the kneebar are essentially the same as for the armbar (juji-gatame). In both cases, it is vital that the joint being attacked (knee or elbow) is above your hips and that you use the insides of your legs to squeeze and control the joint being attacked.

🌀 If you feel as though you are not going to get your hips high enough to submit with the armbar, switch to this technique. It is variously referred to as the **T-** or **L**-sweep and is excellent to use in combination with armlocks because the entry is the same. This technique works well in combination with the basic armbar (pgs. 84-85). Here it is shown as the initial attack. You can also hit it from a failed armbar attempt by taking the leg over their head, kicking down with it, and using it for momentum to sit up. Like all of the sweeps in the last chapter, Blue controls an arm so that White cannot post on it to prevent the sweep.

White's posture is good, as is his base. Blue must change the game to find leverage to make something happen.

Blue reaches under White's leg to help turn himself perpendicular to White. Blue's other hand is cupped behind White's elbow.

Blue pulls with his arm and pivots on his back. At the same time, he is pushing off his left foot to further assist his turn. Blue could turn by pushing off his left foot alone if he wanted.

Blue's right leg comes up high into White's armpit just like he was going for an armbar. His heel is up near White's left shoulder, not down by hips or ribs.

Blue simultaneously pulls on White's right elbow, lifts White's left knee, and bucks the back of his right leg into White's chest. The power comes from Blue's core as he projects his energy into the back of his right leg.

White goes over because he has nothing to post out for base, Blue having control of his right shoulder. As White goes over, Note how Blue comes up on his elbow.

Now Blue can let go with his left hand. Blue pushes off his left elbow and transitions to his palm.

Blue's shins move to either side of White's hips as Blue pushes off his palm.

Blue ends in the mount.

rmbars vs. Stacking:

⟳ When your opponent tries to shift his weight from on top to avoid the armbar, take him that same direction for the finish.

Basic armbar: If your opponent is slow to react, finish with the basic armbar.

armbar

They move forward, over their trapped shoulder: Sweep them over their trapped shoulder by moving your hips that way and pushing with your legs.

They drive forward, over your head: Spin under, head toward first toward their knees. Use your inside arm to push against their leg to help you spin. Finish belly down.

armbar follow-ups

If you don't finish from belly down: Grab their ankle and lift it up and over, putting them on their back.

They move over your inside shoulder (Blue's right): Post off your outside arm and roll over your inside shoulder. If need be, switch to the belly down follow-up above.

They grab your lapel with their free arm: Attack their free arm. Push your own knee and attack the tendon just above the elbow joint.

They grab your lapel with their free arm: Alternatively, you can attack their free arm with the *omo-plata* or use the *omo-plata* as a follow up to the previous technique.

They get their elbow out: Surprise them by switching to a kneebar.

They get their elbow out: As long as you have sleeve control, the *T*-sweep is an option. This works great in combination with the first technique.

CHAPTER 6

ATTACKING UPRIGHT POSTURE

In this chapter, we explore some strategies against an opponent who adopts good posture from his knees. That is to say, an opponent who maintains an upright kneeling position with knees wide, head up, and hands posted on your torso. The top player will take this posture when actively trying to pass the guard. Neither player has an advantage from this position, other things being equal. Do not wait for your opponent to tilt the odds in his favor before making your move.

It can be difficult to attack an opponent who has adopted good posture. The solution is to break his posture down. If your opponent is careless about using his hands and arms to maintain his posture, breaking him down is as easy as pulling him down with a high lapel grip or bucking him forward by pulling your knees toward you chest from the closed guard. Don't forget the simple methods; they are often the best.

Assuming your opponent does post his arms correctly, you will need to deal with them. Some techniques are shown here that start with removing the passing player's arms by first bridging and then pulling on the arms on the way down from the bridge. Do not neglect the bridge (upa) in attempting to remove anchored hands; it is difficult to break grips with your arms alone. Of course, if the passing player is actively attempting to open your guard, he will reposition his hands as the situation dictates. Be ready for the transitions, and when he lets go to move his hands, make your move. The trick with this sort of gambit is to be ready to go right away when the opponent moves without telegraphing your own intent.

Instead of directly trying to break down your opponent's arms by removing them with your hands, you can use your legs to do the work. In the last part of this chapter, Prof. Moreira shows a safe, effective method for using the legs to break down the opponent's base. We call it the Knee in the Chest Series. It has the advantage of requiring very little flexibility for its use.

Once you break down your opponent's base, the odds tip in your favor, and many options present themselves, some of which fill this chapter.

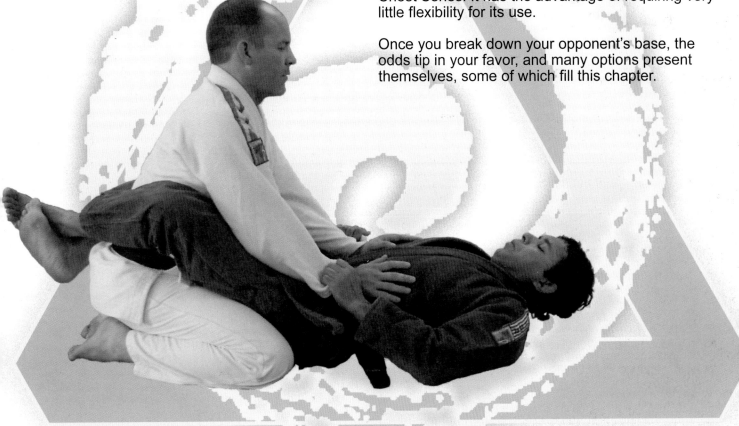

🌀 One of the best ways to break down good posture is to go to work on your opponent's arms. One of the best ways to go to work on their arms is to attack the structural weakness on their elbows, which is to say, push or pull the inside of the elbow away from the opponent's body.

▲▲ In the top row, White's right elbow is inside Blue's left thigh; in the bottom it is outside. Either way, Blue wants to pull it away from White's body.

▲ If White's elbow is to the outside of Blue's leg, Blue reaches over and to the outside of White's elbow with his right hand.

▲ If Blue hides his elbow to the inside of Blue's leg, Blue reaches for White's elbow with both hands.

🌀 It is not so easy to get the wrist lock most of the time. If White moves his palm to escape, Blue follows up.

White frees his hand, but his arm is still vulnerable.

Blue keeps hold of White's elbow. Blue's body blocks White's forearm. Blue moves his leg high up White's back. Blue pushes with his right hand into White's head.

Blue pivots on his back and throws his left shin over and in front of White's head, removing his right hand as he does. Blue's left leg goes over in one big motion.

▲▲ Blue peels White's elbow away from his body. Blue moves his hips out as he does. This gives Blue an angle to use the strength of his body against White's arm.

▲▲ It is hard for White to resist moving in the direction Blue is pulling. White lets things get worse by not taking his palm off Blue's torso.

▲▲ Blue cups his hands around either side of White's elbow and pulls it forward and down. White's hand is bent backward, forcing a wrist lock.

◉ This is known as the *omo plata*. A more detailed explanation of the move is found on pg. 122.

Blue controls White's arm with his own inside (left) hand. Blue uses the sole of his right foot to continue pivoting on his back, his head moving toward White's feet.

As Blue comes around, he straightens his legs to force White's shoulder to the ground. Blue reaches across White's back with his inside arm to keep White from rolling forward.

Blue sits up in an *S-position* with his legs and continues to hold White's back. Blue leans forward, which lifts White's hand up and forces a shoulder lock.

❷ The next four techniques fit together nicely. First is the *Kimura* and then several variations on the hip-bump sweep. In each technique, Blue is once again, one way or another, attacking White's elbow by pressuring the inside of the elbow so that it moves away from White's body. Of course, core body movement is key, but the attack against the inside of the elbow plays an important role in destroying the opponent's base. Be on the lookout for ways to attack the inside of your opponent's elbow when they are in posture.

Normally, in order to get the *Kimura* or hip-bump sweep (next spread) you need one of your opponent's hands on the ground. Experienced opponents are usually cautious and avoid putting their hands on the mat from upright posture in the guard. Nevertheless, it happens, and you can seize the moment. If it does not happen, make it happen. Making it happen can be as simple as quickly pulling their wrist(s) to the side. Over the next four techniques, Blue uses three different approaches to getting White's wrist to the side; each works with all four techniques.

Blue grips White's wrists lightly so as not to telegraph his intention.

Blue pulls White's hands to the mat. Situations may occur where the top player just puts his hands on the mat, though that is a mistake.

Blue takes a figure-four hold on White's wrist. It is very important that he wrap his right arm around above White's elbow and not below.

Blue continues to come forward so that he can have the space to get a solid grip.

Blue holds White's right arm to the ground.

Blue opens his legs, snakes slightly to his right, and sits up.

Blue pulls his chest up to White's right arm and reaches over with his own right arm.

◉ Blue does not put his thumbs around White's wrist or his own.

Blue lifts White's arm while pushing his wrist.

Blue twists his torso back the other way. He keeps a 90-degree bend in White's elbow. His hips snake back to the left; the contact near his left knee helps his hips move.

Blue's left leg keeps White from rolling out of the submission. Blue lifts White's wrist up and toward White's own spine. Blue's forearm holds White's elbow down.

The hip-bump sweep works well in combination with the *Kimura*. Here, it is demonstrated as a follow-up to the *Kimura* when White tries to defend the initial attack by straightening up and back.

White has good posture. Blue's entire back is on the mat; that will not do.

Blue takes hold of White's wrists and raises his hips.

Blue snaps his right hip into White's belly. Blue is posting on his left elbow and right foot at this point, giving his hips a lot of range of motion.

White's reaction keeps Blue from locking the figure-four, but opens up the sweep. Blue lets the figure-four go and repositions his hand for better base.

From this perspective, it is easy to see the circular nature of the sweep. Blue posts on his right foot and opposite (left) elbow, spins his hips, and takes White with him. Note the angle of attack. Blue positions his foot and elbow diagonally when he throws the hip-bump, and White is swept diagonally, not straight to the side.

Blue quickly brings his hips down and a little out, snake-move style. Blue's quick hip movement allows him to better strip White's right hand to the mat.

Blue holds White's right wrist with his left hand and White's shoulder with his right hand, which allows him to use his right arm to come up.

Blue's legs are open as he sits way up. Now Blue reaches deeper with his right hand. White sits up in an attempt to avoid the *Kimura*.

From here, Blue could easily secure the mount position if that is what he wanted.

Not content with the mount position, Blue goes back to work on the submission and takes the figure-four grip.

Blue finishes with the *Kimura*. Blue's right leg is in contact with White's chest. Blue lifts White's shoulder to make space for the shoulder-lock submission.

🌀 This time, White leans into Blue and straightens his arm to stop the Kimura and post against the hip-bump sweep attack.

Blue attempts the hip-bump sweep.

Blue snakes his hips to the right, moving them out from under White's left hand.

Blue pulls White's arm to the side. Blue has to open his legs and commit to the technique if he is going to make it work.

White posts out his hand to stop the sweep.

🌀 White defends the sweep by straightening one arm and blocking Blue's hip with the other.

Blue attempts to sweep White.

White immediately drops his upper body.

White defends by posting out his right hand and blocking Blue's hips from coming up with his left.

Blue hooks in his foot and switches his hand. Instead of pinning White's hand, he will scoop under it.

Blue immediately attacks White's defense by pushing on White's right wrist.

Blue projects himself forward and pulls White's hand off the floor, moving it farther away from White.

Blue sinks in the figure-four. White's arm is straight, so Blue attacks the elbow.

Blue's bottom (right) forearm is below White's elbow. Blue pushes opposite the orientation of White's thumb, hyper extending the elbow.

Blue brings his left hand to his ear and at the same time pulls his head and chest back, extending White.

Blue also straightens White out with the hook. Both Blue's legs control White as he scissors him over.

Blue has the mount. Blue must keep White's head to the outside of his right arm for the finish.

White's arm is there for the taking. Blue makes the figure-four and finishes with the American lock.

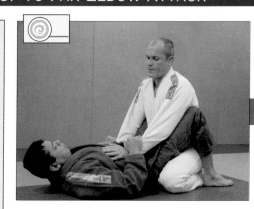

● The next ten techniques work when both the opponent's arms are to one side. One entry into the position is demonstrated, but of course there are many ways you could get to it. For instance, you might get to the position by attempting an arm drag. Recognize the opportunity when it presents itself.

With all of these techniques, it is vital that you trap your opponent's near arm (here, White's right) by bringing your chest tight against it so that the arm is sandwiched tightly between you. That way, you can use both your arms against one of his or against his neck, which is only being defended by his one free arm.

Blue opens his guard, keeping the inside of his legs flush to White's hips as he does.

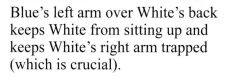

Blue's right arm comes in behind White's far elbow. He still holds White's near arm in the top frame; in the bottom it is already over White's back.

Blue's left arm over White's back keeps White from sitting up and keeps White's right arm trapped (which is crucial).

Blue's right hand is cupping White's left triceps and he pulls his chest in tighter to White, further trapping White's right arm.

Blue lifts his hips. He will bring them back down quickly and out to his left.

As Blue's hips come down, he quickly turns and shoves White's arms to the side, into a 'hole' he has created.

Blue is on his right side, and his legs are open for the moment.

Blue positions the inside edge of his wrist just above White's elbow joint. Blue wraps his head, neck, and shoulder around White's forearm.

Blue holds his hands palm-to-palm. Blue uses his neck and shoulder to pinch White's forearm.

Blue grinds his radius (wrist bone) into the tendon above White's elbow. His whole upper body turns. His legs prevent White from smashing into him and bending his arm as a defense. White's elbow is hyper extended; the pressure on the tendon is no picnic either.

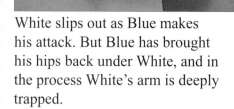

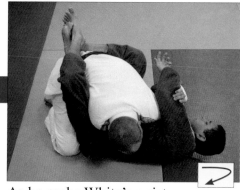

White slips out as Blue makes his attack. But Blue has brought his hips back under White, and in the process White's arm is deeply trapped.

Blue starts adjusting his attack right away. Blue keeps White's elbow pinned with his right wrist and reaches for White's wrist with his left hand.

As he grabs White's wrist with one hand, Blue grabs his own biceps with his other hand.

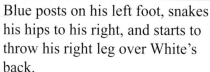

This is a figure-four grip, but opposite the usual *Kimura* hold. This grip is more difficult. Blue will need to reposition himself for the finish. He opens his legs.

Blue posts on his left foot, snakes his hips to his right, and starts to throw his right leg over White's back.

Blue's right leg keeps White from rolling forward. Blue keeps White's elbow at a right angle. Blue keeps himself tight to White's arm as he cranks it back.

White tries to lift his upper body by stepping forward and posting his foot. Blue takes advantage and uses White's posted foot to make adjustments of his own.

As Blue attacks, White posts his foot forward for base.

Blue hooks his right arm under White's raised knee.

Blue pushes White's neck, opens his guard, and spins on his back.

 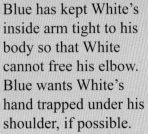  

Blue has kept White's inside arm tight to his body so that White cannot free his elbow. Blue wants White's hand trapped under his shoulder, if possible.

Blue wraps his left leg tightly around White's head, using it to push White's head away. Blue's right leg comes high up White's back into White's armpit.

Blue ups his hips for the finish. This is a very tight armbar. If White had freed his hand from under Blue's right shoulder, Blue might have used a standard armbar (*juji-gatame*).

⊚ If you miss the armbar, go for the kneebar. Since Blue already has a grip around White's knee, he has a good transition to an attack against it.

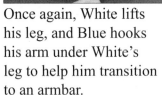

Once again, White lifts his leg, and Blue hooks his arm under White's leg to help him transition to an armbar.

This time, however, White finds space to pull his elbow free.

The armbar is lost; Blue moves on. He pulls his right leg back so that his knee is between White's legs.

Blue pushes White's elbow and clears his other leg.

Blue brings his foot back and over.

Blue snakes his hips and brings White's leg over him. His hips must be above White's kneecap, which is to say toward the thigh, not the shin.

Blue steps on White's calf and continues the lateral movement of his hips.

Blue wraps his arm over the top of White's leg and triangles his feet. Blue only has to lift his hips a bit for the kneebar.

❷ You have many options once you get your opponent's arms to your side. So far, we have seen how to attack either arm and how to go for a kneebar from the position. Here is how to use the position to set up a collar choke.

As before, Blue breaks White's grip by bridging and pushing the arms to the side on the way down.

Remember to move your hips.

Blue switches hands but keeps holding down White's shoulder.

Blue slides in his right hand for the choke.

Blue takes a deep collar grip, four fingers in, with his right hand.

Blue keeps holding White's sleeves as he turns to his side and brings his chest tight to White's right arm and chest.

Blue underhooks White's arm and pulls down on White's shoulder.

Blue is tight against White. Blue starts to cross his legs.

see ch. 3 for more on chokes

The fingers-in lapel grip will keep White from posturing up very far. That allows Blue to let go of White's shoulder and take a thumb in grip with his other hand.

Blue puts on the modified *X*-choke.

Note how Blue rotates his upper body out to finish the choke. First he makes everything tight, and then his torso supplies the power to a very tight choke.

⊚ Pay close attention to the way Blue controls White's arm here. Blue brings his right elbow in front of White's right wrist while Blue's right hand cups White's right elbow. This is a very secure grip and an opportune position from which to switch into the grips for the previous five moves of this series.

Blue bridges his hips and pushes White's arms off to one side on the way down.

The rotation of Blue's torso and a shift of the hips create a "hole" for White to fall into.

Blue's right elbow pushes back at White's right wrist.

Now Blue cups his right hand behind White's right elbow. Blue hangs on White to make White bear Blue's weight.

Blue keeps his elbow to the mat and pulls White's wrist back under him. He keeps his hand cupped around White's elbow as he does.

At this point White is in trouble and posturing will only make things worse.

Blue slides his free arm across White's neck and grabs White's other arm. Pushing away White's head will limit his range of motion.

Blue's right leg keeps White from moving to the side. White's arm needs to stay bent. The finish is similar to an American Lock.

This technique works well if your opponent is trying to pull the arm trapped against your chest up and out; but only if you first get your grip around his far elbow.

Once again, White pulls his right arm free as Blue makes his attack.

Blue's left hand goes over White's back to stop White from lifting up to soon.

Blue needs to keep control of White's left arm. Blue begins to pivot on his hip while pulling on White's left elbow.

As White postures, Blue redirects his motion by pushing White's head. Blue rolls from his side to his back. He uses the pushing and pulling of his arms to help spin himself on his back.

Blue throws his leg over White's shoulder.

Blue straightens his leg as he turns parallel to White. Straightening the legs helps drive White's shoulder to the mat.

Blue sits up and holds White at the hips. His kneecaps go from pointing away from White's head to pointing toward it.

Blue bends his knees, keeps White's butt down, and leans forward for the *omo plata*.

❷ This time, White counter-attacks as Blue tries to use one of the previous techniques. White pushes down Blue's knee and moves forward to pass. As White comes forward, Blue will circle to White's back. The key is to post on the elbow and then the palm of the hand.

Blue is on his side with a grip on White's back and both White's arms to one side.

White pins Blue's leg and steps over.

Blue moves his chest over White's head.

Blue brings his right leg over.

Blue begins to hook in his foot.

Here, instead of dragging White on top of him, Blue climbs onto White's back.

Blue pulls down on White with one arm and slides his elbow back, as if tracing an arc.

Blue comes up on his elbow. His hips slide away from White also.

Blue posts on his palm. His palm plants where his elbow was, or even further back. Blue posts on his left foot and opposite hand (right).

As his left hook moves in, Blue also dives his left hand under White's armpit.

Blue feels that White is leaning to his right. Blue projects himself diagonally forward over his shoulder.

White is never able to fix his right arm, so Blue pulls White back over White's trapped right shoulder.

⊘ This time, White quickly resets his posture to defend. But since he relies on posting on his extended right hand, Blue has another option. Instead of coming up and taking White's back, Blue attacks belly-down for the armbar.

Blue has White's arm in a dangerous position.

White manages to lift up enough to post his hand on Blue's right knee.

White shoves down Blue's knee so he can base out his left leg.

In the top row, Blue was already on his right elbow, and now he drops (the better way). In the bottom row, Blue just now gets on his elbow.

Blue drops his right elbow back and behind. He pivots on his shoulder and swings his leg over. Most of his weight is on his shoulder.

Blue holds White's trapped right arm tight to his chest. With his other hand he pushes White's head away.

Blue's shin slides into the space he created by pushing White's head. His shin then takes over pushing White's head.

Blue makes sure his knees are tight as he wraps up with both hands and finishes the armbar belly-down.

☯ Use this technique when your opponent commits to moving far off to your side to counter your position. This one needs to be a bit of a surprise, so be careful not to telegraph your intentions.

Once again, White tries to pass over Blue's leg.

As White tries to pass, Blue puts his Achilles into the bend of White's leg. His grip on White's back helps him maintain the right position.

Blue triangles his legs.

Blue sits up to the side of White and sinks his shin in deep behind White's knee.

Blue brings his right arm up and over as he sits all the way up.

Blue scoops up White's foot with both hands.

Blue leans back and at the same time pushes his shin forward and down into White's knee. The finish is a keylock to the knee.

⊚ Knee in the Chest: Here, we begin a new series of moves. The last series of attacks all involved first pulling down the opponent and attacking from the side, on your side. In this series, the attacks still involve attacking from the side, on your side, but here they begin with pushing the opponent away.

Blue holds White's right elbow

Blue holds both White's elbows

Blue pushes into White's chest with one hand and holds White's elbow with the other.

The push keeps White from coming forward and allows Blue to move back. Blue snakes his hips out just a bit as he pushes.

Blue has made space to bring his knee under White's arm. Blue puts his foot in White's hip and uses that as a purchase point.

Blue snakes his hips out. Blue steps his right foot on White's hip, which helps Blue adjust his hips.

⊚ Sometimes when you go for the straight armbar (above), your opponent will defend by rotating his arm to take away. By gripping your palm against his, you can attack the elbow and/or shoulder.

As Blue attempts the armbar, White defends his arm by dropping his elbow to the mat and turning his wrist clockwise so that the back of his hand is toward Blue.

White continues his defense by grabbing his own wrist so that it will be difficult for Blue to straighten the arm.

Blue continues to keep White from coming forward because his foot is blocking White's hip.

Blue pulls on White's elbow as he turns to his side. Blue uses his right hand to block White from bending his arm. Blue brings his left knee over the top of White's shoulder. Blue's right leg stops White from coming forward.

Blue will wind up at a right angle to White.

Blue's shin pushes into White's face, taking away space and range of motion in White's extended right shoulder.

Blue levers his knee up while moving his hips forward and his upper body back for the armbar. Blue is mindful of the direction of White's thumb and pulls the opposite way.

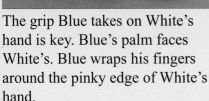

The grip Blue takes on White's hand is key. Blue's palm faces White's. Blue wraps his fingers around the pinky edge of White's hand.

Blue pulls White's hand back to crank White's elbow and/ or shoulder. Blue pulls in the direction of White's thumb.

Blue rocks his left shoulder back for more power. White's left-hand grip is no match for the power from Blue's torso.

> ⌾ This time, as Blue puts on the armbar from the first move in the series, White rotates his wrist the opposite way. When he does, he gives Blue the *omo plata*.

As Blue brings his leg in front of White's face, White defends by turning his arm so that his thumb goes toward the mat.

White's arm is turned the wrong way for Blue to finish from here.

Blue removes his bottom leg from White's hip and begins the transition to *omo plata*. He still uses one arm to control White's arm.

Blue holds White's belt. Blue's left leg keeps pressure on White's shoulder. Blue straightens his legs and sits up. At this point he can release the grips he has on White's arm.

Only once he has sat up does Blue switch the direction of his knees back toward White.

Blue sits forward to apply the shoulder lock. Usually this is enough for the submission, but White has flexible shoulders.

Blue scoops under White's arm.

Blue uses his free hand to pull White's wrist to the other side of his head.

Blue uses his neck and shoulder to pinch White's wrist. Blue holds his hands palm-to-palm and grinds the thumb edge of his wrist into the tendon above White's elbow.

Blue does not get his left knee over White's shoulder fast enough. White pulls up; Blue switches to a standard armbar.

This time, White lifts his left shoulder before Blue can push it down with his knee.

Blue maintains a grip on White's right arm with his right arm so his left hand can move to the left side of White's head.

Blue spins one way and pushes White's head the other. Blue's inside (right) leg comes up high into White's armpit.

White cannot drop down because Blue's hand is on his neck.

As Blue's leg comes in front of White's face, it pushes White's head away.

Both Blue's legs wrap around White. By curling his legs around White's neck and back, Blue helps lift his own hips to finish the armbar. Blue can make a much tighter armbar with this type of leg positioning than with crossed feet.

🌀 Take what your opponent gives you. In the last three techniques, Blue attacked White's right arm. This time, White is quick to hide his right elbow. But when he does, he drops his head, giving Blue an entry into the half-triangle.

▶ ▶ ▶ ▶ Blue moves his knee into White's chest, preparing to attack.

White is trying to drive forward. Blue uses a straight-arm to deflect him, making space to bring his right knee under White's armpit.

Blue uses both hands to control White's arm.

White pulls his elbow back in an effort to defend. The back of White's head is in reach.

Blue takes his foot off White's hip as he pulls White down by the neck.

Blue's left forearm in White's neck keeps space between himself and White.

Blue's left forearm in White's neck keeps space between himself and White.

Blue takes a figure-four grip. His right wrist is just above White's elbow joint.

Blue straightens his torso. As he does, his right hip pushes into his own arm to make more pressure into White's elbow. This is an attack to the elbow.

Once Blue's knee is in front of White's chest, White can no longer drive forward.

With his right knee in White's chest and his right hand on White's left elbow, Blue is able to move White's left shoulder --and White with it.

Blue snakes his hips left, and White's base is disrupted. Once White's posture is disrupted, Blue begins switching grips with his right hand.

Blue's leg comes over White's shoulder. Higher is better. **The back of Blue's leg must be over the top of White's shoulder.**

White's arm is still in position enough to stop Blue's triangle. While the triangle is not an option, a half-triangle attack is.

Blue pushes on White's shoulder and crosses his right leg on top of his left foot.

The "half triangle" is a good position for a number of attacks.

With the half-triangle, you must push your opponent away with the backs of your legs while simultaneously containing him with your crossed ankles.

If White postures, Blue can attack the elbow (pictured). Once it gets to this point, White is hard pressed to drop down.

If White turns to his right, he gives Blue the *omo plata* (next spread).

If White turns to his left, he exposes himself to the triangle and/or *juji-gatame* armbar.

Blue has White in the half-triangle. White defends by twisting his left arm clockwise, dropping his head as he does. Blue's first response is to move to the *omo plata*. White counters by holding the back of his own leg. Blue is able to flip White because White refuses to let go of his own leg. Blue finishes by pulling up on White's elbow while White's arm is trapped under Blue's hip.

*A detailed description of this attack from the **omo plata** appears on pg. 156.*

White holds the back of his own leg.

Blue's left leg begins to move under White's head.

Blue's upper body continues to rotate.

Blue cups White's head with his left hand allowing Blue to move his hips closer.

White's left hand is stuck under Blue's right hip.

Blue crosses his ankles.

Blue lifts with both hands against White's elbow: shoulder crank.

◎ Can you see how this finish might also be used as a follow-up to a failed triangle choke attempt?

In this scenario, Blue again attempts to move to the *omo plata* from the knee in chest guard. As he does, White reacts differently. Instead of dropping his left shoulder and twisting his arm, White pushes his right hand into Blue's gut to fix his posture. When White does, he gives Blue the angle to put both his legs on top of White's shoulders for a double armbar.

This time, White pulls his elbow free before Blue can off-balance him.

Blue begins to take advantage of White's compromised posture. He crunches to his right so that he brings himself under White's arm.

Blue switches from pulling on White's arm to pushing it. The back of Blue's leg comes over White's shoulder.

Blue shoots his legs through and brings his hips toward White's chest. He pushes off his side/shoulder to propel himself.

Blue crosses his feet and uses his legs to pull himself tighter to White. White is concerned about a half-triangle attack. White straightens up to defend.

Blue maintains control of both White's arms. White pushes forward to avoid the half triangle.

Blue lifts his other leg over White's shoulder.

Blue crosses his feet, hugs White's arms, and lifts his hips for a double armbar. Blue pushes his knees together as he extends. Both of White's elbows are submitted.

Attacking Upright Posture

◉ *Attacking your opponent's elbow is a good way to break down upright base, especially if their hands are to the sides of your hips.*

elbow attacks

Their elbow to the outside of your legs: Pull their elbow out, then push it back into your stomach for a wrist lock.

They move their hand to defend the wristlock: Continue to pull their elbow away from them. Take advantage of their broken posture and bent elbow by attacking with the *omo plata*.

They post their hand: Their hand might get to the mat as a defense to the above techniques, or otherwise. Whatever the case, attack with the *Kimura*.

Their hand is on the mat and their posture is high: Attack with the hip bump; sink in the figure-four on the way over, and finish with the *Kimura*.

They post their hand against the hip-bump: Reap their planted hand with your hands, taking their base and finishing the sweep.

They post their hand against the hip bump: Like above, reap their planted hand with your hands. Switch to a butterfly hook to finish the sweep.

◉ *Try to get both of your opponent's arms to one side of your body, then hold down the far shoulder and attack.*

far elbow attacks

Entry: Bridge your hips. Drop your hips quickly and push both their arms to one side. Wrap your arms around their far shoulder as your chest traps their arm.

If they post out their far arm: Wrap your arms around their far shoulder as your chest blocks their near arm. Your neck and shoulder trap their wrist. Your radial bone presses above the tendon above the elbow.

Their palm turns up: Pull their elbow to your chest then use a figure-four grip to apply the reverse *Kimura*.

(cont'd)

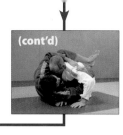

far elbow attacks

They step forward: Scoop under that leg, push their head, and attack their near arm with an armbar.

They pull their arm free: Slide your inside knee between their legs, and go to the kneebar.

They posture: Your inside hand grabs their lapel, four fingers in. The top hand grips thumb-in. Make an X-choke.

Attack the near arm: Your bottom elbow pulls back their wrist. Your top arm goes from holding their waist to driving in front of their chest.

They posture: Pull their far arm to your chest. Push their head and go to *omo plata*.

they push your leg down

Take the back 1: Come up on your elbow and off to the side. Step over and put in your hook. If they lean into you as you do, pull them back toward you.

Take the back 2: Same as above, but pull yourself on top and take the back from there.

Attack their arm: Consider this if they post their near arm. Make sure you pivot on your shoulder.

The truck driver: This needs to be a surprise. Sit up high and make sure your shin is deep in the crease of their knee from the beginning.

☯ Rather than attacking your opponent's arms, put a knee in their chest and use the power of your legs to break down their posture.

knee in chest series

Knee in chest entry: Straight arm their chest with one arm. The same side knee comes under their armpit then pushes their chest. Hold their sleeves and use your knee to disrupt their posture.

Step over to armbar: The top knee presses down their upper arm as the lower leg swings in front of their face and then pushes their face. Pay attention to the orientation of their elbow and pull that way.

They turn their arm up: Your top hand grabs their trapped hand, palm to palm. Pull their hand. The attack is similar to an *Americana*.

They turn their arm down: Pull your bottom leg out and transition to the *omo plata*.

They lift their head: Grab the lapel opposite the arm you are attacking, straight arm, and pivot on your back as your outside leg swings around their head and you set an armbar.

They pull their elbow back, head low: Grab the back of their head and bring your same side leg on top of their shoulder. Your inside leg goes back under their armpit. Cross your feet, bolt-lock

They twist out of the half-triangle: Switch to the *omo plata*. If they defend by grabbing their own leg, go to your hands and knees, forcing them to roll. If their hand ends under your hip, lift that elbow.

They shove their arm back in to defend the half-triangle: Lift your hips high. The backs of your legs go on top of their shoulders, cross your feet and hit the double armbar.

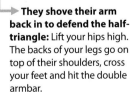

CHAPTER 7

ATTACKING A STALLING POSTURE

It is inevitable that you will encounter opponents and training partners who adopt a very defensive posture that involves placing their head on your stomach and holding their elbows tightly to your sides or hips. Players usually take this position in order to catch their breath and/or stall. Regardless of anyone's opinion on the tactic, it is a fact of life in grappling and mixed martial arts. Because the top player is so low to the mat, it is difficult to off-balance him from this position. His arm and neck are seemingly hidden. Compounding the situation, he may have fairly good control of your hips.

Here we will look at ways to attack the three most likely variations on the stalling posture. The first two spreads in this chapter show techniques for attacking a stalling posture where the opponent holds at your sides. Later in the chapter are techniques for contending with an opponent who tries to stall by holding the biceps. Finally, an option is shown for times when the opponent tries to stall holding his arms more on top of you than to the sides. Even if you are unable to finish the techniques, they will get your opponent out of his stalling posture, thereby opening other opportunities.

Regardless of the stalling posture used, Prof. Moreira's counters all have one thing in common: they use big muscle groups to attack smaller ones. In that regard, the approach is the same as for any other position in BJJ.

Once you take your opponent out of the stalling posture, all sorts of possibilities open up. The last technique in this chapter flows into the first of the next. So it is on the mat; one thing leads to another.

Drill the stalling posture. Have your training partner start the drill locked down as best he can. Your objective for two minutes is to make something happen. His is to stall. This is an example of position-specific training. It is very beneficial, because it allows you to focus your concentration on one specific position and to attempt things you might not otherwise be willing to try for fear of getting in a tight spot should you fail.

Additional attacks against stalling posture appear in Ch. 3, *Chokes*, and Ch. 8, *Flowing Attack*.

❷ Attacking a defensive posture requires creating openings in the opponent's defenses. Blue uses his torso and legs to create an angle for attacking White's elbow. White's elbow cannot resist the power of the snake move.

White is clamped down in a stalling defensive posture.

Blue pushes the back of White's head and shifts his hips the opposite way.

Blue cups both hands around White's elbow. Blue is going to attack with the *Kimura*. The *omo plata* is a good option from here also.

Blue uses his body core and legs for power as he pulls White's elbow to his chest.

White defends by lifting his leg and hooking it with his palm. This creates a brace that prevents Blue from lifting White's wrist.

Blue uses his whole body against White's hand. Blue pushes White's lower body one way and pulls his arm another.

White's wrist is not strong enough to counter Blue's torso, and he losese his defensive grip.

Blue repositions his foot and snakes his hip out further.

Now Blue has space to put his foot in White's hip. By doing so, his thigh forces White's elbow up. Even if White let go, his arm would be in danger.

By holding on, White has left his elbow exposed. Blue begins to establish a hold behind White's elbow.

Blue never lets White's elbow move off his chest. He controls the elbow with his right hand and then immediately grabs White's wrist with his left hand.

As Blue slides his right arm through for the figure-four, he never lets White's arm get away from his chest. Blue crunches forward to make getting the grip easier.

With the grip set, Blue puts his leg over to stop any rolling escape and lifts up White's wrist for the *Kimura*- style shoulder lock.

Blue keeps White's shoulder low and brings his wrist high.

White is in the same position as in the previous technique.

Bluc pushes White's head with both hands and uses that to help him reposition his upper body.

Blue keeps pushing with his left arm as he replaces his right hand with the back of his right elbow.

Blue has moved his hips away from White's elbow and in doing so made a gap. Blue slides his left hand into the gap.

> ❂ When in the guard, if you can pry your opponent's elbow away from his body, you can go on the offensive. Your chances of sucess are better if you can keep your opponent guessing what is next. This time, instead of getting behind White's elbow and pulling it forward, Blue attacks it from the front and then locks his hands behind White's elbow to drag it forward. He stil attacks White's same elbow, though, this time with the reverse *Kimura*.

> Your range of motion when applying the reverse *Kimura* is pretty limited. If your opponent is able to resist the initial application, you can create more range of motion by moving off to the side. It will be necessary to take your leg off his back to do so. Once you are off to the side, you need to counter rolling escapes by throwing your leg over his back again.

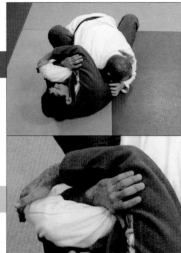
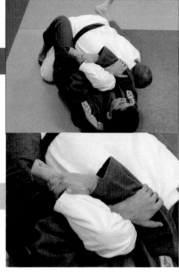
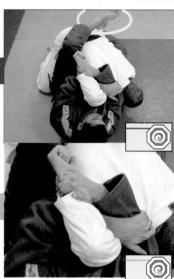

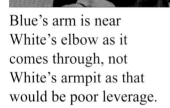

Blue's arm is near White's elbow as it comes through, not White's armpit as that would be poor leverage.

Blue reaches for his own biceps and White's wrist.

Blue takes a reverse figure-four. Blue snakes his hips back under White and out the other side. Blue has only to keep his grip secure, and his body movement will force up White's arm.

▲ Blue uses his posted left foot to push off for his snake move.

▲ Blue uses his left leg as purchase to move his hips.

Blue lifts White's wrist with his arms and keeps White's back down with his leg. Blue needs to keep White from grabbing his own gi as he does. This is a shoulder lock similar to the *Kimura,* except that the grip is reversed.

White escapes the submission by straightening out his arm.

Once White frees his arm, Blue is no longer concerned that White will lift his hips to relieve the pressure. Blue posts his left foot on the mat so he can reposition his hips.

Blue keeps his left arm tight to White's elbow, just above the joint, and turns his upper body.

White twists his arm free by moving his thumb up.

Blue is ready. With his left arm, he keeps Whites elbow tight and grabs White's wrist with his right hand. Blue moves his leg over White's back.

Blue transitions into a figure-four American Lock.

◉ The reverse *Kimura* can be difficult to maintain. You need to be prepared to transition to something else should your opponent slip free. Blue is ready with multiple follow-ups should White power out of the submission.

Blue comes up onto his elbow and snakes his hips away from White. Blue's left arm grabs his right lapel.

Using the space created by the elbow snake move, Blue puts both of his feet into White's hips. He does not want White to be able to defend by smashing forward. Blue moves his upper body away from White.

Blue pinches White's wrist between his neck and shoulder. The submission can come two ways. Blue can hyperextend White's elbow and/ or create pain at the end of White's triceps tendon with the blade of his wrist.

◉ This time, as he breaks out of the reverse *Kimura,* White rotates his arm in the direction opposite the technique above. Blue is ready; he imediately goes for the *Americana*. Note that both Blue's arms are to the same side of White's head; this is vital to the success of the tecnique.

It is vital that Blue bring his right elbow to the outside of White's head. Blue's right foot impedes White from coming forward.

Blue has shifted his hips. He crunches forward to torque White's arm and finish the shoulder lock.

❷ Never forget the basics. White manages to make his way out of the reverse *Kimura* and the elbow lock. But Blue never lets White's arm free. The result is that even after escaping the first two submissions, Blue is in a position to follow up with a basic armbar.

White escapes the elbow attack again. This time, he drops his arm and elbow down as he twists his arm out of the elbow attack. Blue immediately comes off of his elbow and wraps both of his arms around White's arm. Blue switches his right foot from White's hip to near his knee. Blue wants to flatten White.

The inside of Blue's thigh is tight to White's shoulder as it comes over the top. That takes away space White needs to free his elbow and keeps him flattened.

Blue's knee comes to the side of White's face. He never lets the pressure off White's shoulder as his upper leg rotates over.

Blue holds White's forearm to his chest, moves his hips forward, and levers his knee off his toes into White's head.

Having just put in a word for the basics, we switch gears. As your game progresses it is handy to have some suprise moves. It is equally if not more important to recognize "trick" moves so that you are prepared to avoid them. There is value to learning techniques even if you never use them so that you are aware of them should they be attempted on you.

This move is not likely to catch an opponent who is looking for it. But with so many possible moves from the guard, it is difficult to be on the alert for all of them.

White is holding Blue's biceps and attempting to stall or catch his breath.

Blue notes the direction White is looking and starts to snake the other direction. Blue comes onto his side and brings his left elbow up and over.

Blue wants White's hand near White's thumb to get stuck between Blue's biceps and pectorals. Blue holds his own elbow to make things tighter. At the same time, the top of his thigh jams against the back of White's elbow, blocking his escape route.

The trap is sprung. Blue continues to twist his upper body and simultaneously crunches forward. The back of White's hand is cranked back and twisted for a wristlock.

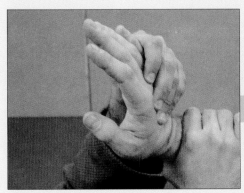
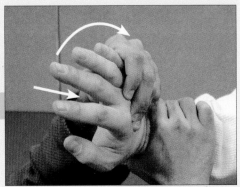

The action of the wrist lock is to twist the hand so that the pinky side rotates up...

...and the back of the hand is forced toward the forearm.

☯ The way Blue traps White's hand here is similar to the way he did so in the last technique. Instead of using the hold on the hand to apply a wristlock, Blue uses it to set up an armbar.

White holds at the biceps and will not let go.

Blue lifts his arms, thereby extending White's. Blue repositions his left foot and snakes his hips out just a bit.

Blue uses the space he just created to put his left foot on White's hip.

Blue puts his other (right) foot on White's other hip. Blue brings his left elbow up and over, grabbing his sleeve with his other hand as he does. White's hand is stuck and his arm gets twisted as Blue turns. That causes him to drop his head, thereby exposing his arm to attack.

The wristlock is not making White tap. Blue adjusts his grip so that his left hand cups White's wrist. Blue tries to prevent White from rotating his thumb by holding tight. Blue brings his left knee over tight to White's shoulder to keep White from posturing.

Blue crosses his arms over White's, pinning it tight to his chest. Blue could bring his top leg in front of White's face but opts instead to apply the finish from where his leg already is. Blue squeezes his knees together and pushes White's head away with his top leg. White's thumb is pointed away from Blue's chest. This is an armbar variation.

Attack the back of their elbow (entry): Push their head and snake a little the other way. Use the top of your thigh to open up their elbow, then pull it from behind with both hands.

Kimura: Now that you have opened up their elbow, the opening is there for the *Kimura*.

They counter by grabbing their leg: Use your core strength to break their grip. Hug their arm tight to your chest, push with the back of your leg, and rotate your upper body.

Attack their elbow from the front (entry): Push their head to make space, then block their head with your elbow. Swim the other arm under their shoulder, then clasp your hands and pull.

Reverse *Kimura*: Make a figure-four grip with your hands reversed from the regular *Kimura*. Move your hips under the attacked arm, then block their hips with the back of your leg.

They straighten their arm: Never let the back of their elbow free. Snake away, catch their wrist between your neck and shoulder, and push down on their shoulder with your knee as you extend.

They turn their elbow down: Switch to the *Americana*. As with any *Americana*, their head cannot be inside your figure-four grip.

They pull their hand out: Use an armbar. Make sure your knee keeps their shoulder down as your lower leg comes in front of their head.

Attack their wrist: If their hands are on your biceps, take advantage of the fact their arms are extended. Trap their hand against your pectorals and twist your body to twist their wrist.

They survive: If you don't get the wrist lock, once again hit the armbar. Finish with your legs positioned as shown here, or as in the technique two rows above.

Attacking Stalling Posture

CHAPTER 8

FLOWING ATTACK

The ability to flow seamlessly from one attack into another is a hallmark of high-level jiu-jitsu. You attack, and your opponent counters. If you can anticipate his counter, you can spring a trap. Sometimes it comes down to making one attack after another until you make a decisive move or your opponent runs out of answers.

In this chapter, Prof. Moreira demonstrates some of the combinations he uses from the guard. Of course, there are many other combinations; the number of possible submission combinations is limited only by our imaginations. As your jiu-jitsu improves, you will learn games and combinations that work well for you.

As the title suggests, the theme here is flowing from one attack to another. The sequences start with a triangle attack against an opponent holding the knees. We could have started from just about any technique, but as you might notice, the first technique connects with the last from the previous chapters. The order of the techniques is not the point; the idea is to give the reader some insights into how to connect various techniques.

When you practice the techniques, variations in your execution or your partner's reactions will invariably arise such that it might be better to flow in a different direction. So be it; jiu-jitsu is a dynamic art well adapted to addressing unexpected variables. You attack, your opponent counters, when he counters, something else opens up, you attack that opening. If you can stay a step ahead so that your opponent is struggling just to catch up, you are likely to get your submission after a few tries. If not, keep trying. Persistence is key on many levels, and by this we don't refer to belt levels, though progressing to higher belt levels is itself also largely a matter of persistence.

The sequences here necessarily follow a particular order or else they could not be set to print—or

any other medium. In a live situation, we do not know how things will play out; neither do you or your opponent. The question arises: Is it better to have a set plan, or is it better to react to the moment? The answer is some mixture of both. If you rely too heavily on a set plan of action, you run the risk of becoming lost when the unexpected happens—and it will—or when you fail to execute as you had planned—and you will. Reacting to the situation at hand allows for the possibility of adapting to the unexpected and taking what the opponent gives. But if you do not already know what to do during the brief time an opening presents itself, the opportunity will be lost before you can react.

Opportunity favors the prepared. To seize upon a momentary opening, you must already have the basic mechanics and coordination of your move ingrained in your mind. Flowing attack requires a mixture of close attention to the moment, analysis, and ability to react 'without thinking.' At a high level, it is not that you are not thinking, but that you no longer have to think about all the various elements required for the precise execution of a technique.

Practice creating a flow of techniques by training with a partner, both of you only using 50% or less of your strength. Take turns going on the offensive. At the same time, attempt to make good technical escapes. When you get to a point where you have a submission, back off and move to another, or allow your partner to mount a defense, and continue from there. Both players should be scoring points and arriving at finishing holds. In order to get maximum benefit from this sort of practice, there needs to be give and take by both players. Understand that the goal of the drill is recognizing and executing technique in a dynamic situation. Keep the drill non-competitive so that neither of you is reluctant to go for techniques you might not otherwise attempt for fear of putting yourself in a bad situation.

❂ White is stalling, just like in the previous chapter. This time, his hands are on Blue's chest. His elbows are to the outsides of Blue's legs. As the sequence begins, it is important that Blue's legs not be loose against White's sides. Blue does not need to squeeze hard, but he needs to keep firm pressure so that White is not free to move any which way and so that he can feel which way White is intending to move.

Blue pushes on White's left wrist and simultaneously snakes his butt slightly to that same side. Blue holds White's other arm in place.

Without letting go of White's wrists, Blue throws his right leg over White's left shoulder.

Blue reaches across and holds behind White's elbow. Blue wants to pull White's elbow back across his body.

Blue uses his left thigh to block White from pulling back his right elbow, the one Blue wants to attack. Blue pushes off with his left foot to help turn his upper body.

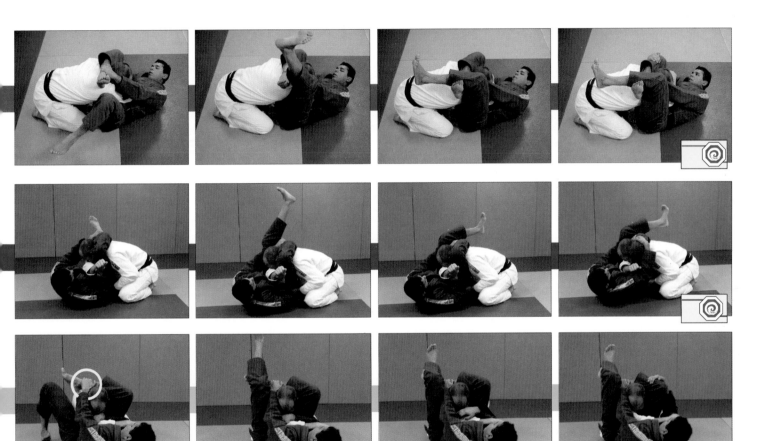

Blue keeps turning until his shin is in line with a line from one of White's shoulders to the other. The back of Blue's leg bites into White's neck.

Blue's free leg comes up and over his bottom leg. Blue holds his shin with his left hand so that White does not get loose in the process.

Blue will make a tighter choke if he flexes his toes toward his shin as opposed to pointing them. Keeping the feet bent tenses the calf muscles for extra pressure, as does curling back the toes.

To finish the choke, Blue pulls on his own knee and White's head. He squeezes his knees and pushes from his hips.

❂ The triangle is an excellent finish. Even so, it does not always work. Blue is prepared to follow up without missing a beat. If White protects his neck, Blue attacks his arm.

White is resisting the choke. Blue's left hand pulls his right shin and he adjusts his hips trying to finish White. Blue right hand grabs White's right hand.

Blue has already tightened his legs and adjusted his hips, so he no longer needs to hold his shin. Blue slips his left hand under White's wrist.

❂ This time, White stands up, and his elbow is no longer lodged against Blue for the wristlock. White is getting out. Blue does not insist on the triangle any longer once he knows White is bound to escape. Blue feels the moment and changes from pulling White's head down with his leg to pushing it with his arm.

Use the opponent's own force against him.

White comes to his feet and begins to twist free.

Blue knows the triangle is lost. He readies his arm for the next attack.

Blue makes a small, tight, figure-four grip.

Blue bends White's wrist in the direction of White's elbow. Blue has White's elbow with his left leg: wristlock.

As White pulls away, Blue wedges the edge of his wrist into the side of White's head. Blue braces his hand against his leg. This keeps White from smashing back down.

There is just enough space for Blue to find purchase for his left leg on the side of White's head. First, the shin comes in near the ankle, and then he pushes up his leg.

Blue needs to be conscious of the alignment of White's arm and move his hips accordingly. Blue needs to finish from here right away, or White will escape.

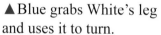

Before Blue can finish, White twists his elbow free.

White needs to lean and push into Blue to make power to free his arm.

▲ Blue pushes off the mat with his left hand to help himself turn.
▲ Blue grabs White's leg and uses it to turn.

Blue pushes White's shoulder to the mat and orients his own hips towards the ceiling.

🌀 **Above:** In Chapter 5: *Armbars vs. Stacking*, we saw a number of options for finishing the armbar depending on the way your opponent reacted; this spread begins with a technique that could have appeared there. In the technique above, White reacts to Blue's armbar by shifting his upper body over Blue's right shoulder. Blue decides that he is better off staying on his back instead of going belly down for the armbar, because White has managed to duck his head around Blue's left leg.

🌀 **Below:** In the second technique, White counters the omo plata above. Blue realizes that he has missed the *omo plata* and immediately hits the shin-in-armbar.

This time, Blue does not control White's back in time, and White rolls out of the *omo plata*.

Blue is using his left arm to hold White's right leg. He uses his right hand to grab the belt and pull himself up.

Blue's feet move in arcs as his knees drop. His legs come to an "S" position away from White.

Blue brings his left arm over for more control. Most of his weight is on his chest and the knee that is over White's shoulder.

It does not matter which side of Blue's body White's trapped arm is on; the *omo plata* works either way.

Blue is ready. As White rolls, Blue is unencumbered in his own transition.

Blue is careful to keep his hips below White's elbow. The sole of his left foot is on the mat as he presses the back of it into White's face.

Blue pushes his knees together. Everything is tight, including his right leg against White's side. Blue turns White's thumb to the ceiling and lifts his hips into White's elbow.

⊙ In the last technique, Blue finished with an armbar variation where his left leg was across White's face but his right was not across White's body, but bent, shin in the ribs. This sort of armbar is frequently attempted in conjunction with judo throws: a forward hip throw, for instance. It a good technique to use after a throw because you can enter into the armbar quickly. The weakness of the technique is that there is an opportunity for your opponent to spin out over his shoulder. Here is the counter to that escape.

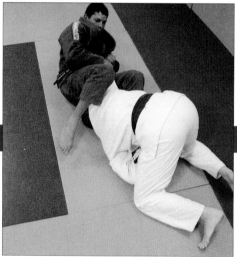

White knows he has a chance to roll out of the armlock, especially this type, where only one of the attacker's legs is across his body.

At this point, Blue needs to switch techniques, or White will come out the back and get superior position. Blue comes up onto his elbow.

Blue brings his top leg over to put in his hook.

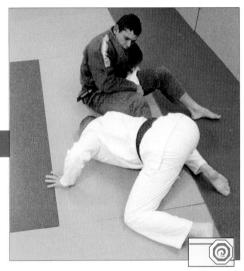

Blue hooks his right instep in White's right thigh and starts to come up on his hand.

Blue posts on his left hand and leg and uses that base to lean into White's shoulder. With Blue sitting on his shoulder, White's arm is trapped.

Blue finishes White by hyper-extending his elbow from here. To make the elbow lock, Blue pushes down with his hooking inside (right) leg. Blue can hold White's belt and/or wrist for extra control. If White turns his elbow out of the lock, it is time to move on to one of the next two techniques.

White turns his elbow out of danger and starts to move toward Blue.

White is able to lift his head and is threatening to pass Blue's guard.

Blue grabs White's belt and keeps pressure on White's elbow.

❷ As seen in the top row: Blue attempted the *omo plata*: White rolled out of it: Blue switched to the shin in the ribs armbar: White rolled out of that: Blue attacked White's shoulder, but White has avoided the submission.

Now: Blue demonstrates two options to continue his attack. **Above:** Blue shows what to do if White lifts his head and tries to smash into Blue. **Below:** White tries to roll out again, and Blue moves into a standard armbar.

White is concerned about Blue's right hook.

White rolls over his inside (right) shoulder to escape.

White reaches behind Blue's back to take pressure off his trapped arm and position himself to pass the guard.

Now White has no base under his left shoulder. He is a table with one leg missing. Blue pulls on the belt and elevates with his right leg, which is hooked between White's legs.

Blue pushes off the mat with his left foot as he leans back and pulls. From here, Blue has an easy transition to side control, or he could go to the next technique.

Blue grabs White's belt to control where White rolls and to keep him from making too much space. ▲ Blue slides his leg over White's chest as he rolls.

Blue pulls on White's arm to extend it. Doing so also helps him bring his hips closer. Blue brings a leg over White's head.

White has rolled into an armbar.

White defends the armbar by pushing Blue's leg off of his head.

White continues his defense by trying to put his head on Blue's leg.

Blue begins to counter. Blue lifts his right leg and starts to move his foot around White's head. Because White has lifted his head as part of this defense, there is some space behind his neck that Blue can use against him.

> ☯ Now we continue from the armbar attempt shown at the bottom of the last spread. White tries a common defense: With his free (left) arm he pushes Blue's top (left) leg off his head and attempts to get his head and shoulders on top of Blue's top leg.

Blue presses his right instep firmly behind the base of White's neck.

Blue's right shin also makes pressure on the side of White's face, pushing White's head away. White's escape from here is to sit up, but Blue is about to shut that down.

Blue brings his outside (left) shin in front of White's face, below the chin. He finishes with his feet scissoring White's head, his thighs tight to White's arm, and White's thumb up. Blue must push his knees tightly together to immobilize White's arm and finish the submission. Blue pushes in the direction opposite of White's thumb to lock White's elbow.

Blue's feet control either side of White's head and arm.

⊘ The armbar variation on the last page requires a bit of finesse. If you do not get the armbar right away, your opponent has a chance to escape by pushing your top leg (Blue's left in the photos) over his head. If he does, his next move will typically be to sit up. When he sits up, he will let go of your foot. That is your chance to hit the triangle.

This time, White defends by pushing the leg across his body and over his head.

White sits up and attempts to pass Blue's guard. Blue must maintain control of White's trapped arm.

Blue must be quick. Instead of trying to keep White down with his leg, Blue quickly moves it in front of White's head.

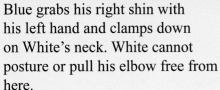

Blue grabs his right shin with his left hand and clamps down on White's neck. White cannot posture or pull his elbow free from here.

Blue brings his other leg up high. If he could, he would like to bring it down with some impetus to make the triangle tighter.

Blue has the option of continuing to hold his shin or letting go. This time, he holds. With White's arm across his body the way it is, it will be easy for Blue to execute the triangle. Blue lifts his hips and squeezes his legs for the finish.

☯ Note that we are back where we started, with Blue making the triangle attack. Sometimes that's how it is…you try something but at first it does not work…you make the best of changes in the situation again and again…you get what you wanted!

❷ This is the beginning of a new sequence of attack techniques. Once again, the first move is a triangle choke. Remember, the idea behind showing these sequences is to give you some insight into how to connect various techniques. Here we are connecting submission attempts. By throwing one submission attempt after another at your opponent, you put your adversary on the defense. Sooner or later, if you can keep on the attack, you should get something.

Blue is attempting to control White by holding White's sleeves.

White breaks his hands free.

White holds the cloth at the inside of Blue's knees with the intent of passing guard.

Blue sits back, using his upper body momentum and falling weight to remove White's hand.

Blue's right hand (not visible) is blocking White's left forearm as Blue pulls his right knee through.

Blue hooks his leg over the back of White's neck. The back of his leg helps knock White down, as does stretching him out.

White jumps back and drives Blue's feet to the floor.

Blue sits up and wraps his hand around White's right arm.

Blue brings his body close to White's arm. He cups his hand around White's forearm.

Blue's bottom leg has been keeping White away. Blue will now use that space to pull his leg out. Blue pulls White's arm across his chest.

Blue's right leg is high on White's back and White's arm is pulled across his own body. It will be easy to make a tight triangle from here.

Blue squeezes his knees together and pulls down on the back of White's head to finish the triangle.

◉ In the first series of techniques, White tried to defend the triangle by raising his hips (pg. 138). This time, White is a little quicker to defend and postures out of the attack. Unlike in the previous spread, Blue is unable to secure the triangle tightly. But Blue still has a good position for attacking White's trapped right arm.

Blue goes for the triangle.

White uses his trapped right arm to push. Blue is unable to sink in a deep triangle hold. Blue is controlling White's left wrist. This prevents White from grabbing Blue's lapel near Blue's neck to help him smash down on Blue.

White's posture prevents Blue from finishing the triangle. In his effort to escape, however, White has straightened his right arm. Blue seizes the opportunity and pushes White's arm to Blue's left side.

Blue swims his left arm in front of White's right hand and traps it Blue's left armpit. Blue tightens things up immediately. His left arm holds outside his left knee and assists it in pushing into the back of White's elbow.

Blue holds his own leg and extends his hip in the direction opposite the direction White's elbow bends. Blue pushes White's knee to help prevent White from coming forward to make space to escape. The submission hyper-extends the elbow if White does not tap.

Blue attempts the same submission as in the previous spread.

White defends the elbow attack by twisting his arm counter-clockwise.

Blue attacks the back of White's elbow, pulling it forward. He uses both his arms against one of White's, uncrossing his legs in the process. Blue keeps White's back down with his left leg.

The easiest escape from the last technique is for White to twist his right arm to take the pressure off of his elbow. The downside, for White, is that when he does so, he leaves his elbow in a compromised position, vulnerable to the *omo plata* or *Kimura*. Here, Blue opts for the *Kimura* first, but the *omo plata* is there if he wants it right off the bat or as a follow-up to the *Kimura* (next spread).

Blue holds White's wrist and begins to come over the top of White's elbow. White's arm must stay bent.

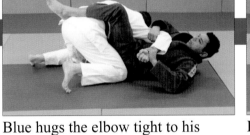

Blue hugs the elbow tight to his body with one arm and grabs White's wrist with the other.

Blue takes the figure four grip. He pushes into White with the back of his thigh as he does. This helps prevent White from grabbing material to defend.

Blue lifts up White's wrist while keeping White's elbow down.

Blue pulls the elbow toward him and pushes the wrist away. His right hand begins to thread its way to his left wrist.

As his hand slides through, Blue does not give White a chance to fix his arm.

Blue does not wrap his thumb around his wrist. To finish, Blue will pull White's elbow to his chest and lift White's wrist.

❷ This technique works from either the *Kimura* or the *omo plata*. It is used when the opponent grips his own gi and/or the inside of his thigh to block a *Kimura* or *omo plata* attempt. It is especially useful if the opponent refuses to let go of the grip on his own leg. If he does let go as you begin to turn, pull out your bottom leg and switch back to *omo plata*.

White has a secure grip on his own leg, protecting his shoulder.

▼Blue drops his left leg so that his foot is a bit under White's head.

Blue rolls to his side, posts on his elbow, and transitions to his palms.

Blue's lower body follows his upper body.

See also pg. 126.

White is forced over by his own defense.

Blue keeps his spin going. He will drop to an elbow and then to his side.

At this point, White will not be able to keep his grip. His insistence on trying has left his hand trapped under Blue's hip.

Blue crosses his feet around White's head and pulls up with both hands on White's elbow. The result is a shoulder crank.

◎ Blue sees one opening after another with the irreplaceable aid of experience. He has done the moves so many times that he does not have to think much about the mechanics of his execution. This is not to say that he is not thinking; to the contrary, he concentrates intensely as he rolls. His knowledge of the physical movements allows him to focus on seeing entries, sensing opportunities, timing, and fakes. Jiu-jitsu is in the mind!

White's arm comes free. White might escape, or maybe he is mindful not to let Blue pin White's arm with his hip as they roll.

White twists his arm counter-clockwise and pulls away.

Blue pulls White's arm while at the same time curling his right leg over White's chest.

Blue puts his other (left) leg in front of White's face. White's elbow is above Blue's legs and Blue has tight control of White's arm. Because White's thumb is pointing to Blue's right, Blue will finish the armbar by pushing the opposite way, to his left.

❷ This time, White defends Blue's armbar by blocking Blue's leg from coming over in the first place. The players might also get to this position if White makes this defense to a basic armbar (juji-gatame).

White fends off Blue's left leg and puts his head on top of it to defend against the armbar.

Blue brings his right leg to the near side of White's face. He blocks White with one arm and keeps hold of White's arm with the other hand.

❷ This variation of the armlock above has the advantage of providing more control over the opponent's head.

Blue can feel that his hips are still above White's elbow, so he continues to attack.

Blue's right shin is tight to White's neck.

Blue lifts his other knee. Both his feet are under White's head, and he pushes his knees together.

Blue is attentive to the direction of White's elbow (or the direction of White's thumb) as he pulls back for the armbar.

See also pg. 156.

Blue uses both his hands to control the position of White's hand.

Blue uses his left foot under White's chin as a lever. As always, Blue makes the hold tight by squeezing his legs together.

❷ It is better not to show your opponent the same move twice. Continuing from the spread on **pg. 156**, Blue decides to use a different method for dealing with White holding his own leg to defend. Instead of attempting a sweep, Blue attempts a figure-four footlock.

Blue is in a position to apply the *Kimura* (shoulder lock).

White raises his hips and steps forward with his right foot.

White grabs behind his leg to stop Blue's submission attempt.

Blue lets go of the figure-four grip but not White's wrist. With his right hand, Blue pushes White's head away; this helps position Blue to put his leg over.

Blue puts his leg over and to the side of White's head as if he is going for the *omo plata*.

Blue puts his left shin on the right side of White's face. Once his left shin is in place, he posts on his right foot and moves his hips away from White.

Instead of reaching up and grabbing White's back, Blue reaches under and around White's leg.

Blue stretches out White. He takes a figure-four grip on White's foot. Blue will keep White's leg close to his chest and extend the foot to finish the submission.

White defends the footlock by putting weight onto his foot, thus stopping Blue from extending it.

Blue abandons the footlock. His inside (left) arm blocks White's hip, preventing White from stepping over him.

Blue proceeds to an *omo plata* attack. He pushes White's shoulder to the ground with his left leg. Blue's elbow helps him rise.

❂ There are many options from the *omo plata* setup.
Above: Blue transitions from the figure-four-toe hold to the *omo plata*. He could also have gone from the *omo plata* to the figure-four toe hold.
Right: White is not submitted by the basic *omo plata,* so Blue attacks White's free (left) arm.

White is resilient in resisting the *omo plata*. Blue lifts White's arm at the biceps.

With his other hand, Blue pulls up White's forearm.

Blue sits up and uses his left arm to prevent White from rolling forward.

Blue wants to move his hips away from White's torso at this point. In the top row, Blue is basing on his palm to assist his hip movement.

Blue turns his legs to an *S* position and leans forward to finish the *omo plata* shoulder lock.

The side of Blue's face traps White's arm.

Blue grinds his wrist bone (the same part of the arm he would use for a choke) into the tendon between White's triceps and elbow.

↻ As one door closes, another opens. White frees his arm from the *omo plata* but exposes his neck in the process.

Blue slips his hand under White's arm, and he grabs White's lapel.

The first hand in pulls the slack out of the lapel and pulls it just away from White's body. This makes it easy for Blue to slip in the other hand and take a deep collar grip.

Blue can ▲ grab the wrist or ▲ base his hand on the mat. Blue's base is wide, and his weight is on White's back.

As Blue sits up, White pulls his arm free.

Even though White's arm is free, Blue still has the better position.

Blue presses his advantage. He immediately brings his chest to White's back, hips to White's hips.

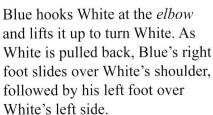

Blue steps forward and raises his body.

Blue hooks White at the *elbow* and lifts it up to turn White. As White is pulled back, Blue's right foot slides over White's shoulder, followed by his left foot over White's left side.

This is known in judo as the *hell-choke*. Blue simultaneously pulls White's arm and lapel. Blue pushes White's shoulder away with his bottom leg, resulting in a very powerful choke.

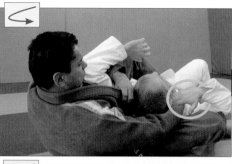

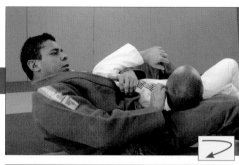

This is the last technique of the second flow of submission techniques. It is pretty unlikely in actual combat that you will ever go from beginning to end in the exact order we have shown. But that was never the point. Practicing going from one submission to another is a good idea for many reasons, not the least of which are building muscle memory/coordination and developing awareness. Most of the time, techniques are not pulled off the way you first learn them. Take the armbar, for example. Sometimes you can get it just the way you first learned it from the guard. But most of the time your opponent puts up some sort of defense to your first attack and then you attack with something else. If you can keep your opponent on the defensive as you throw one thing after another at them, chances are something good is going to happen for you. Practice going from one technique to another cooperatively and you become more aware of what is possible while training your body to move at the same time.

White manages to stave off the *hell-choke*. White uses his elbow to keep Blue's leg off his shoulder while taking pressure off his neck by pulling on Blue's arm.

Blue's right arm pushes White's head one way, which in turn helps Blue rotate his upper body the other. Blue's left arm grips White's left arm; this helps him keep control of White's elbow.

Blue throws his leg over for the armbar.

Blue's right arm scoops under White's left arm at the wrist.

Blue leans back and applies juji-gatame. Blue's right leg is tight around White's head.

Triangle: First hold their arm, then, with your other hand, hold your own shin. Keep the balls of your feet pulled back.

Wrist lock: Take advantage of the control you have over the back of their elbow. Use a figure-four grip to attack their wrist.

○ The point is not to memorize a long series of moves. The point is to develop the awareness, coordination, and habit of moving from one attack to another.

Armbar: They pull their elbow free by twisting away from you. This is a good angle for the armbar with both legs over the shoulder of their free arm.

Omo-plata: If they push back into you with their head, go with it, switching to the omo plata.

Armbar: If they roll out of the omo plata, keep control of their arm, as their back hits the mat, switch to the shin-in-the-side style armbar.

Elbow attack: If they make to roll out escape to the shin-in-the-side armbar, step over in front of them, slip the hook in, and go for the elbow attack.

Sweep: If they posture up and twist their elbow free, grab their belt and go for the sweep.

Armbar: Look for the armbar from the sweep.

Armbar: If they defend by pushing your leg off their face, switch to your other shin behind their head then cross your other leg over their face.

Triangle: If they sit up, switch back to the triangle as they come up. Now you are back where you started, but with the triangle against their other arm.

@ **This time, the opponent defends the initial triangle attack differently. The series of attacks that follows differs accordingly. Take what your opponent gives you.**

▶ **Entry and triangle:** If they are upright and post their hand on the inside of your knee, cup their forearm or elbow, pull as you lean back, and figure-four your legs.

▶ **Triangle to armbar:** If they posture out of the triangle, trap the front of their arm in your armpit; straighten your hips to finish the armbar.

▶ **Armbar to *Kimura*:** If they twist their arm forward to escape the armbar, turn to their side, grab a figure-four grip, and use the *Kimura*.

▶ ***Kimura* to *omo plata* sweep/attack:** If they defend the omo plata by holding the inside of their own leg, go to your hands first, then twist your lower body. Lift their elbow if their hand is trapped under you.

▶ **Elbow attack to armbar:** If they get their hand out from underneath you, go to a standard armbar.

▶ **Armbar to armbar:** If they push your leg off their head, use this variation with your shins crossed and insteps around their head.

🌀 *Here we see an alternate path that might develop from the Kimura attack. Every step of the way, there are different things either player could do that would change each other's reactions. Practice following the flows, but as you see other possibilities, explore them and develop new sequences.*

Kimura to *omo plata* (foot lock): If your opponent holds his leg to defend the *omo plata*, another option is to switch to the omo plata. If they still hold on, attack their foot/ankle.

Foot lock to *omo plata*: If they get the sole of their foot to the mat in defense, control their hips with your arm and go back to the *omo plata*.

***Omo plata* to elbow attack:** If you are having trouble finishing the *omo plata*, attack their other arm by trapping it between your neck and shoulder and putting pressure on their tendon with your wrist bones.

Hell-choke as a counter: If they pull their arm out of the *omo-plata*, switch your base so your chest is to their back, grab their lapel with your top hand, and feed it to your bottom. Sit back to the hell-choke.

Hell choke to armbar: Release the lapel, then push their head away and put on the armbar.

CHAPTER 9

NECK AND HEAD CONTROL

A grappling cliché is that if you control your opponent's head, you control his body. It is not as simple as that, of course, but there is a lot to be said for controlling the head from certain positions, the guard included.

All of the techniques in this chapter involve establishing control over the back of the opponent's neck and pushing his head down with either your arms or your torso. From there, you must control one or both of your opponent's arms. Opportunities for these types of attacks typically arise when the top player lowers his head while trying to pass the guard, by going over or around one of your legs. These moves are also effective right after a single-leg takedown, if the opponent keeps holding your leg after you go to the mat. The threat of these moves is an argument for good posture while passing the guard. Good posture will prevent your opponent from using these moves to trap your neck and/or head.

The first sequence of moves involves going to the crucifix position. Be careful not to get dumped forward when you are on top in the crucifix position. If you feel that starting to happen, give up whatever submission attempt you are in the midst of in favor of keeping the better position. The second sequence is done from the guard position and involves a similar method for controlling the opponent's neck. In either case, stay tight and maintain control over at least one of the opponent's arms. The two main ways an opponent will defend are by holding his arms together or by backing away to free his neck. Be mindful of his defenses, and stop them before they progress.

Brazilian jiu-jitsu competition rules have started to gravitate toward forbidding neck cranks, presumably because of the potential for serious injury. That being said, be very careful with any sort of attack to the spine. Injuries to the spine tend to be permanent. That is not a lesson you or your partner wants to learn the hard way.

⊙ As usual, hip movement is key. First, Blue draws back his right elbow in an arc and posts on it. Then he pushes off his left foot as he snakes back his hips. Next, he posts on the palm of his right hand and his opposite (left) foot. Blue lifts his hips, pulls back his bottom (right) leg and rotates his body from the hips. This is the snake move he will use to transition to the crucifix position.

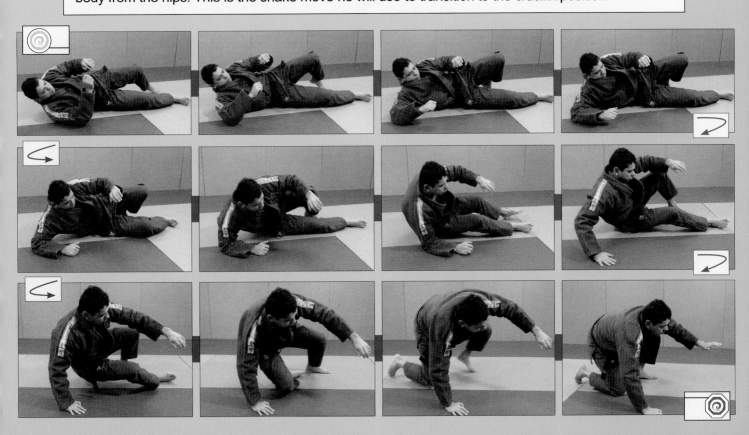

White pushes down Blue's left leg and steps over.

White starts to underhook Blue's right leg.

Blue comes up on his left elbow while pushing on White's head. Blue posts on his right foot and slides his hip back in the process.

⊚ White passes one of his legs over Blue's leg and brings one of his arms between White's legs. Blue takes advantage of the situation. The key, of course, is hip movement. Blue makes the snake move from the preceding page.

Blue moves himself belly-down across White's shoulders. Because White put his arm between Blue's legs, White's arm gets scooped up by Blue's left leg as he turns onto his knees and goes belly-down onto White's shoulders.

Blue has White in the crucifix position. From here, he can roll White over (see next spread), attack his arm (next frame), or work a choke.

⊚ ►►► From this angle, you can see clearly the similarity to the elbow-to-palm snake move.

Now Blue has space to hook his right foot in front of White's thigh.

Blue post on his palm and grabs White's belt. Blue unhooks his left leg and pulls it out from between White's legs at the same time that he hooks in his right foot.

Blue comes up onto the palm of his left hand, arm straight. Blue curls his left leg so that his heel moves under his butt.

Blue brings his right foot under his left. If White leaves his arm straight, Blue can curl his legs back for an elbow lock.

If White uses both arms to hold one of Blue's legs, as might be the case after executing a single-leg takedown, there are several ways Blue might attack White's arm. On this page, we see the attack if White keeps his arm straight when Blue goes to his back. If White defends by turning his arm one way or the other to defend, Blue will use the techniques on the next two pages.

↻ White defends the elbow lock (previous technique) by turning his palm to the mat and bending his elbow. Blue counters by sliding one knee under, pulling back his other leg, and thrusting his hips forward. The result is a shoulder lock like the *American lock*.

Slide the bottom knee in front of the top knee and under the arm.

Use pressure from the hips to keep the opponent's chest to the mat.

The players start in the same position as the last technique. This time, White defends by turning his arm the opposite way. White turns his palm up and bends his elbow. Blue turns his hips accordingly. This time, the submission is a shoulder lock similar to the *Kimura*.

White turns his palm to the ceiling and bends his elbow.

Blue turns his hips, following the direction into which White has rotated his arm. As Blue turns, he uses his hips to drop his weight on White's head. Blue does not want White to roll out of the submission.

Once again, Blue brings the bottom leg under and the top leg back. Blue finishes the submission on either his elbow or palm. The finishing action is a shoulder crank similar to the *omo plata*.

❷ Sometimes the opponent escapes the previous technique (shoulder lock) by rolling forward; sometimes the opponent has flexible shoulders and can withstand the pressure. Either way, there is an easy transition to the crucifix position.

Sensing that the shoulder lock is not going to work, Blue grabs White's belt so that he can have some control over White's hips.

Maybe White jumps over, or maybe Blue pulls him over. Either way, as White goes over, Blue makes sure he wraps his left arm around White's free right arm.

Blue lets go of the belt with his right hand and transitions to grabbing White's lapel. Blue's right leg pulls back on White's left arm as his left pushes forward, keeping White's left arm securely trapped.

Once Blue has the lapel grip with his right hand, he uses it to feed the lapel to his left hand, which reaches across White's throat.

Note how Blue pulls out all of the slack so that he can get a deep grip in the lapel with his other hand.

Blue slides his right hand in behind White's head, back of the hand to White's head and fingers straight. The choke is executed by pulling the lapel, slicing down with the straight hand, and pulling back a bit with the legs.

❷ In the first move of this chapter (pg. 184), as Blue transitioned from countering White's guard pass attempt to getting on top of White's back, Blue was able to hook one of White's arm in the process. Suppose that White moves his arm to avoid that, or suppose that Blue arrives at attacking White's turtle position a different way: now Blue is in position to attack with the crucifix.

Blue takes his right hand and reaches across White's neck, grabbing White's left lapel. From here, Blue might attack with the clock choke. However, White is posting on his right hand and is beginning to lift up, making the clock choke difficult. White's defense creates space Blue can use to hook White's right arm with Blue's right foot, which he does.

Blue's left hand scoops under White's left armpit and the palm of Blue's hand grips the front of White's left shoulder.

Blue lifts with his right leg and moves his left foot forward and under White's right arm.

❷ It is better to get the lapel grip before turning over your opponent, but it is not strictly necessary.

*More finishing moves from the crucifix position appear in **Passing the Guard**: Vol. 1, Ch. 7, of this series:*

Blue kicks up his non-hooking (left) leg up to create momentum to roll himself and White. Blue drops his upper body as he does, he will roll over his left shoulder.

Blue a grip on White's lapel provides control and is the beginning of a choke hold. Blue could also roll first and then get the grip. Blue's left hand stops White from simply rolling on top of Blue's legs.

As soon as the roll is complete, Blue crosses his feet to better control White's arm. Again, if White keeps his arm straight, Blue can submit him by the elbow. Blue also has a single-wing collar choke in place.

☯ Roll over your shoulder and keep your chest tight to their back as you do.

⊙ Blue has put White into the crucifix position and on his back. As is so often the case, sometimes the initial attack does not work for one reason or another. Here, Blue transitions to a neck crank. If that fails, it is easy to imagine him transitioning to side control.

Blue has the single-wing choke but is having a hard time finishing.

White wants to bring his right arm to his side to stop Blue from attempting the choke again.

White grabs Blue's left hand to defend against other chokes.

Blue has let go of White's wrist with one hand (left) and grabbed it with the other (right). Blue is careful to keep squeezing his knees together and extending White's arm between his legs.

Blue pivots on his right elbow and opposite (left) foot. His bottom leg scoops White's left arm back as he twists his lower body so that his hips turn toward the mat.

Blue can undo the triangle with his legs, but he must keep the bottom, hooking leg bent and White's arms trapped.

Blue lets go of the lapel grip with his left hand and with his right hand grabs White's wrist.

Blue begins to turn farther onto his side.

Blue's top (right) arm comes around White's arm.

It is okay for Blue's hips to come up, but there must be pressure on White's head so that he cannot slip free.

Blue uses his right hand for base and his left arm to pull White's elbow back.

Blue goes back to a triangle with his legs. Pulling White's arms one way and pushing his head the other creates a neck crank. Blue pushes on his right hand to rotate his torso into White's head.
▲ With White's arm the way it is, Blue might also make him tap by lifting up his feet to create a shoulder crank.

❷ Blue uses the Elbow & Palm Snake
Move from pg. 12 to set up this technique.

White is attempting to pass over Blue's leg and into side control.

Blue repositions his right foot, draws his left elbow back in an arc, and comes up onto his elbow. Blue's right palm begins to push the left side of White's face.

Blue snakes his hips away from White while pushing White's head. This makes space that Blue will use to hook in his right foot. Blue's right hand continues pushing the side of White's face.

Blue wants to sit straight up and bring his chest tight against White's face at the same time. He can ▲push on White's head or ▲pull on his belt. Either way, Blue wants White's head off to his left side.

Blue scoops up White's right arm at the elbow with his left arm. Blue will have a shorter lever and need more power if he lifts near White's shoulder. The back of his hand is straight, so it slides through better.

Blue clasps his hands, palm-to-palm, and pulls White's elbow up and over.

Blue puts in his hook as he moves his hips away from White, thanks to using his elbow to aid pulling himself away.

Blue goes from his elbow to his palm.

Blue moves his hips back under White by planting his weight on his palm and lifting his butt slightly off the mat. As he moves his hips back under White, his left knee comes out to the side.

Blue's right foot pushes White's knee as Blue twists White.

Blue stays tight to White as they roll over.

Blue still has White's neck and arm tied up, and he comes up to the mount. If no neck cranks are allowed, Blue will let it go with his left arm and work from the mount.

⊚ Sometimes your opponent can base with his lower body to stop the last technique. Here, Blue destroys that defense by kicking out White's knee.

Blue puts his right foot on White's knee and hooks White's leg with his left.

Blue pushes off his right foot into White's knee to aid the sweep as he elevates White and twists.

Blue is unable to finish the reverse *Kimura*. This might happen because White is flexible or manages to grab hold of his gi.

Blue removes his left leg from White's leg.

Both of Blue's feet come to the mat; the left foot goes back and to his side.

Blue keeps the back of his arm tight to the back of White's head as he rolls into the mount.

Blue pulls up on White's arms and into the back of White's head. The finish is a neck crank. Blue pulls back with his heels to tighten the crank and for added power.

◉ Blue either feels that White's base is too solid or that he wants to trick White by switching tactics. Instead of trying to lift against White's legs, Blue turns White over by continuing to torque White's shoulders. Toward that end, Blue brings his left foot away from White's hips and off to the side, and then posts on it.

Blue posts on his left foot and twists to the side.

The reversal ends with White in the crucifix hold.

Blue hooks his top leg over his bottom leg. He turns to his knees, forcing his hip into the back of White's head. Blue wants his hips up off the mat a bit. The result is a painful neck crank.

White starts to pass over Blue's leg but lowers his head as he does.

Blue comes up on his elbow and pushes the back of White's head.

Blue makes space so that he can put in his right hook (not pictured; see previous spread).

Blue lifts White's arm at the elbow. Blue straightens the back of his hand while sliding it under the elbow.

Blue takes a reverse figure-four grip and cups White's elbow.

Blue makes White submit by pulling White's elbow behind White's back. The awkward position of White's head is key.

❷ From this view, we see how Blue uses his feet when applying either of the two finishes above. White could take pressure off his shoulder to survive the submission if he were to raise his hips. Blue negates that by using his legs against White's.

Blue comes up on his left palm while continuing to push White's head with his right.

Blue moves his hips toward his posted palm.

Blue moves White's head to the side.

> ☷ Once again, Blue uses the Elbow & Palm Snake Move from pg. 12 to set up his technique.

If Blue cannot pull White's elbow back, he can follow up with the reverse *Kimura*.

When applying the reverse *Kimura,* do not let your opponent grab his own gi to defend.

Blue keeps White's head trapped under his armpit as he pulls White's elbow to his head and White's wrist behind White's back.

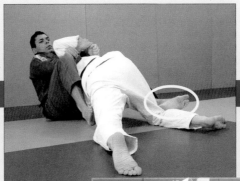

▲ ▸ Blue holds down White's right leg, as he attacks the right arm. This takes away some of White's range of motion to resist the submission.

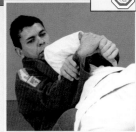

❂ White feels Blue trying to trap his neck and counters. White bases on the palm of his hand to make more power to lift his head. But by putting his hand on the mat, White opens himself up to the *Kimura*. The entry into the *Kimura* is an easy one because Blue is sitting up already.

Use the palm to move the hips.

Blue is already up on his elbow. Blue pushes White's head and snakes away so that White's head is no longer over his hips.

Blue finishes his first snake movement. ▲In the top row, Blue is about to go to his palm. ▲In the bottom row, he is already on his palm.

Blue shifts weight onto his left palm, helping him unweight his hips.

White tries to stop Blue by posting on his right hand to fix his base. Blue's left hand grabs White's right wrist. He slips his right hand over the back of White's neck and uses it to pull himself around.

❂ Sometimes you will not be able to get around your opponent's head or attack the far-side arm as in the last few techniques. If so, think about switching directions and surprising your opponent. Here, as White worries about his right elbow, which is under attack from Blue's arm, he is unready when Blue attacks White's left arm with his legs.

White hides his elbow effectively.

Blue abruptly changes direction, pushing White's head away. Blue uses his right shin in conjunction with his arms to snake back his hips.

Blue straight-arms the left side of White's head. Blue pulls his bottom knee out once he finishes snaking his hips away.

© Blue uses a figure-four grip. The key to the finish is hip movement. Note how Blue's hips move to one side to set up the hold and then come out to the other as he applies the *Kimura*.

Blue sits into White's posted right arm as he brings his right arm over White's elbow, above the elbow joint.

Blue balances on his left elbow as he sinks in the *Kimura*.

Blue hugs White's elbow tightly to his chest as he lifts White wrist. Blue keeps White's arm bent at a right angle, preventing White from straightening or going the other way and grabbing his gi.

Blue's left leg comes over White's lower back to stop the rolling escape.

Blue is on his side as his upper body moves back and his lower body pivots forward on his left hip.

Blue's right shin pushes the side of White's face as the back of his right leg flattens down White's left shoulder.

Blue swing his ankles in arcs as he sits up and controls White's hips. The *omo plata*!

Neck Control Attacks

◉ *Use these techniques after falling from a single-leg takedown or in the situation depicted.*

▶ **The opponent's entry:** Your opponent manages to control the inside of one of your knees, push it down, and step over it. Before he passes completely, you must hook his other leg, half-guard style.

The moves in the white area concern a scenario where your opponent wraps both arms around one of your legs.

▶ **The snake move:** Get on your side; pull back your elbow; snake your hips back. Base on your palm and opposite foot, pull back your bottom leg.

▶ **The entry move:** Use the entry move but hold their belt with your free hand, and scoop their arm with your bottom leg. Make sure to hook your free leg inside theirs before coming up.

arm attacks

▶ **If they leave their arm straight:** Push down with your hips while curling back your legs to pressure the elbow.

▶ **If they turn their hand forward:** Slide your inside leg under their arm and pull back with your other leg.

▶ **If they turn their hand backward:** Slide your front leg under their arm and pull back with your other leg.

crucifix attacks

▶ **Crucifix entry 1:** This works well if the armbar above fails. Pull on their belt with one arm while you scoop under their shoulder with the other, rolling them over you. Your legs control one of their arms, and one of your arms controls the other.

▶ **Crucifix entry 2:** One of your legs is hooking their arm. Push off with the other leg, roll over the shoulder nearest their feet, scoop their other arm on the way over.

▶ **Finish from the crucifix:** There are a handful of finishing moves from the crucifix. Here we show a neck crank. See also, **Passing the Guard**, Ch. 7: *The Turtle Position*.

The moves in the grey area concern a scenario where your opponent wraps one arm around your waist.

The entry move: Get on your side; pull back your elbow; snake your hips back to make space to hook in your free leg. Hold their belt and sit up to so that their head is to the same side as the leg they stepped over.

Sweep to mount: Trap their head in your armpit, then scoop under their biceps, lifting their elbow. Kick out the knee and roll on top. You are positioned for a neck crank, or simply the mount.

Sweep to crucifix: Use this if their free arm is between your legs. Make the same grip as above. Commit to lifting their elbow up and over, keeping their neck trapped as you go.

If they bury their head: Crank their shoulder with a reverse *Kimura*.

If they pull their head out: Your opponent needs to post off their palm to lift their head effectively. Move around their head to the other side and take the figure-four grip for the *Kimura*.

If you cannot get your grips or around their head: Switch direction and switch to the omo-plata, pushing their head with both your arms to help rotate your body.

CHAPTER 10

BACK-ROLLS AND THE TURTLE POSITION

One way to defend certain guard passes—especially stacking-type passes—is to back-roll and/or go to your knees. This sort of defense can be very effective, or it can take you out of the frying pan and into the fire. The aim of this chapter is to provide options for immediate transition out of a back-roll defense or from the turtle position. The coverage here is limited to situations where both players are still oriented in opposite directions. If you wait for the top player to come to your side or behind you (so that you are both facing the same way), your situation worsens. Try not to let that happen, use the techniques in this chapter while you have the chance. Taking the opportunity while it still exists is an instance of good timing. Timing is key.

You are most likely to get into trouble with the turtle position if you stay in it for any longer than necessary. Your back is exposed once you go to your hands and knees, and if you are not careful, so are your neck and arms. Accordingly, the primary options your opponent has are trying for the back mount position, chokes, and attacks against your arms. For example, with slight variations, most of the material in **Ch. 9, Neck Control Attacks**, works against the turtle position, and so do most of the submissions in **Ch. 11, Snake Knees and Standup**. [More on attacking the turtle position appears in **vol. 1, ch. 7,** of this series: *Passing the Guard*.]

This is not to say that the position is all bad; it's not. There are many ways to turn the tables from a hands-and-knees position, as this chapter demonstrates. A first option is just to keep rolling to your back with the objective of replacing the guard (pg. 192). This works well if the opponent is loose as you back-roll.

In an effort to prevent the guard player from replacing guard off of a back-roll, the top player might stuff the guard player's back as the guard player rolls. The top player does this by using his chest against the guard player's back. The upside for the guard player is that if the top player is not careful, the guard player will have a chance to grab one or both of his opponent's legs and reverse him to his back from the turtle (pg. 196).

That being the case, the top player typically sprawls his legs to keep them out of reach. But the top player only has partial control while he is sprawled and oriented in the opposite direction. To compensate, the top player typically tries to hold with his arms. If he wraps his arms around the guard player, the guard player has a chance to go on the offensive. Most of the chapter deals with this scenario.

In a mixed martial arts or self-defense scenario, the turtle position is a horrible place to stay because there is not much you can do to avoid strikes to the head, or even to know where they are coming from. In a contest without striking, however, the position becomes much more viable.

Whatever the situation, it may be necessary to back-roll or turtle to avoid something worse. In this chapter, Prof. Moreira goes to the turtle as a defense to having his guard passed. Often, players wind up going to the turtle position as part of an escape from side control or the north/south position. However you wind up there, once there, options include immediately transitioning to the guard, transitioning to the opponent's back, attacking the opponent's legs (as in sweeping them), and attacking the opponent's arms.

> ⊘ Blue demonstrates the back-roll and follow-through he uses
> as to stop the guard pass and then counter-attack. Back-rolls as
> a defense come in handy against smashing-type guard passes,
> which is the scenario in the photos in the spreads that follow. It
> works against other passes also. Blue does not stop after he rolls
> over; he immediately positions himself to replace his guard.

Blue is on his back as if in the guard.

Blue throws his legs over by contracting his abs and then kicking from the knees a bit.

Blue looks one way (right) as he rolls over the shoulder he is looking away from (left). The more Blue's ear comes to the shoulder he is not rolling on, the easier it will be for him to roll. Posting on his left palm helps Blue roll.

Here it is again, but over the left shoulder. Posting on opposite limbs is, once again, key.

⊘ The back-roll is an often overlooked basic skill. Do not roll over your head. Rolling over your head is hard on the spine and not effective because it requires too much space. Roll over the shoulder. In order to roll over the shoulder, you must drop your head to one side and relax the neck. Look away from the shoulder you roll over. Refine your back-roll until it is smooth.

Blue lands with one knee bent, (the same-side knee) as the shoulder he rolled over (both right). His other leg (left) is outstretched to the side. His non-posting left hand is out in front of him so he can use it to block his opponent from coming forward.

Blue carries his weight on his right palm and opposite left foot. His other foot (right) traces an arc as it comes out from under.

Blue continues back to the starting position.

⊙ The back-roll is a useful defense against being stacked in the guard. Here we see a defensive use of the back-roll. Once you roll to your knees, do not stay there. Although you have many options, as the pages ahead detail, it is a very vulnerable position.

White is stacking Blue. Blue must make his move before White smashes Blue's left leg too far down. Blue starts by pushing off with his left leg against White's right shoulder and kicking his free (right) leg back to generate momentum.

The coordinated effort of both legs makes space and momentum. Blue's head is to the same side as the leg that was trapped as he rolls over his right shoulder. His left palm posts on the mat.

Blue lands on his right knee and left foot. His hips are high at this point, allowing him space under his own hips to maneuver in.

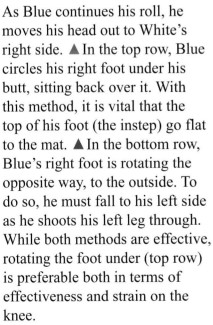

As Blue continues his roll, he moves his head out to White's right side. ▲ In the top row, Blue circles his right foot under his butt, sitting back over it. With this method, it is vital that the top of his foot (the instep) go flat to the mat. ▲ In the bottom row, Blue's right foot is rotating the opposite way, to the outside. To do so, he must fall to his left side as he shoots his left leg through. While both methods are effective, rotating the foot under (top row) is preferable both in terms of effectiveness and strain on the knee.

Because Blue's head is out to the side, there is nothing to prevent him from continuing to sit back. Blue's left foot blocks White's right knee. If White tries to go the other way (if White tries to circle clockwise, for Blue's back), White exposes his back to Blue.

Blue has both feet on White's knees as he returns to guard. Right now would be a good time to try sweeping White over his extended right side. Blue might have also transitioned into the standard or butterfly guard as he finished the back-roll.

🌀 This back-roll series works best if White is committed to pushing forward as he passes. If White does not, Blue runs a greater risk of White stuffing the back-roll. If Blue does not sense that White is committed to coming forward, he must try something else. White sits up high and allows Blue space; Blue continues to play from his guard.

White lifts Blue, but there is space between White's chest and Blue.

One foot goes to White's biceps, and the other comes down over White's elbow. Blue is holding onto both of White's sleeves.

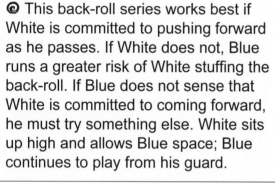

By grabbing his own shin, Blue prevents White from fixing his posture and allows himself the opportunity to adjust his hips without losing the control he has over White's neck and left shoulder.

Blue pulls tight with his arms for the triangle finish. Note that he keeps his feet bent, not pointed.

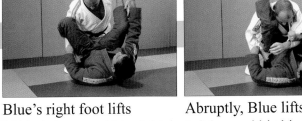

Blue's right foot lifts White's arm, and his right hand pulls the opposite way. Thus, Blue tilts White's upper body.

Abruptly, Blue lifts his left leg and his hips. He snaps his right leg out behind White's left arm and up.

As he lifts his hips, Blue pulls White's arm across.

The higher Blue gets his hips, the better he can bite down with his leg across the back of White's neck.

White manages to withstand the triangle.

White lifts his head.

Blue has White's arm trapped and so lets White pick his poison. Blue holds White's head so that he cannot come back down to defend his arm.

Blue submits White with an armbar by lifting his hips and clamping down with the back of his arm on White's wrist.

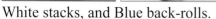

White stacks, and Blue back-rolls.

Before picking up his hand, Blue has switched the knee and foot that are on the ground and has posted his foot to the opposite side of his head relative to White.

Blue drives his shoulder into White while circling his lower body. As he makes his turn, he pulls on White's far knee.

> ◉ This is similar to the move above, but easier. The difference is that Blue's head is on the opposite side of White's body. Instead of hopping over White's leg, Blue simply drives him to the mat and moves directly into side control.

Blue uses his arm and chest to make pressure on White's top leg, preventing White from hooking Blue with that leg to save the guard.

Blue makes a small hop to clear White's legs. Blue does not jump way up, because that would make space for White to fix himself.

Blue maintains contact and pressure with his chest all the way around. Blue ends in side control.

▽ ▼ ▷ ▶ Blue has taken a big step forward with his right foot. His hands come together, and he scoops White's knee from down low while pushing with his head into White's side from up high. Blue makes a quarter turn while executing the sweep. His right knee drops down as he lifts his left knee.

White wraps his left arm around Blue as Blue rolls over. Blue grabs the sleeve and holds tight. Blue will lift his knee and drop his weight into White's arm.

Blue sits out. During the sit-out, Blue pivots from his elbow and opposite foot. Blue makes certain his head is off to the side, not stuck under White's belly.

As White's back hits the mat, Blue wraps his free arm around White's elbow so that White cannot pull it free.

❷ Blue can make a similar move by holding with his other arm as he sits out. Since he is holding with the opposite arm, he must also switch the hand he uses for base to sit out. The key to gripping White's arm with this variation is to wrap around to the outside and above the opponent's elbow and pinch your own elbow back tightly to your side.

◎ The next four techniques all work off the wrestler's sit-out. We recommend learning them together and paying attention to the different options you have depending on what your opponent does with his arms. In the two techniques on this page, Blue attacks White's left arm. This is because White puts that arm in deep as he tries to control Blue as Blue goes to his knees. On the next spread, Blue does not attack White's arms. Instead, he does a sit-out and attacks White's back. After that, on pgs. 218-219, Blue attacks White's right arm with the sit-out. So then, Blue has the option of attacking either of White's arms, or neither of them, depending on what White gives him.

Blue reverses his sit-out. He puts some of his weight into White's wrist as he does.

Blue has a figure-four grip.

Blue immediately brings one knee tight to the side of White's head and the other to White's hip. Blue keeps White's head outside of the figure-four grip as he lifts White's elbow for the armlock.

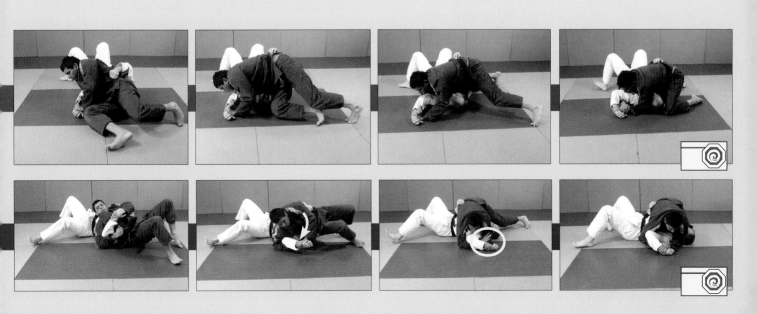

❷ A wrestler's sit-out is an effective move from the turtle position. Again, key elements include getting the head out to the side and making a pendulum action by basing on an elbow and the opposite foot. As the lower body comes forward, the upper body twists back.

If your neck is getting jammed when executing this move, the problem is that you need to move your head out farther to the side. You should be pushing your opponent with your upper back and lower neck, but not carrying his weight with them, and especially not off the back of your head.

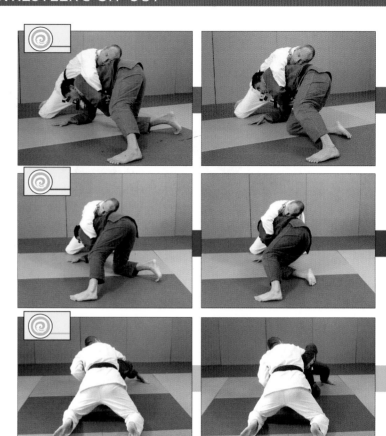

Blue posts on his right elbow and left foot.

He traps White's arm to his side.

▶ ▶ ▶ As Blue turns the corner to White's back, the right side of his chest stays on White's back. Blue post his right knee just in front of White's right knee as he throws his left leg over and sinks in the hook. Note that he never steps his left foot between White's legs.

Blue's bottom leg shoots through.

Once Blue sits through, he will immediately step over with his right foot. Blue brings his left arm up as he sits through.

Blue pivots on his neck and his knee.

Blue's head moves behind White's right shoulder as Blue's right shoulder drives White forward.

❷ This is a variation on the wrestler's sit-out; instead of turning back into White after sitting out, Blue goes straight for the submission. On pgs. 214-215, Blue attacked the arm opposite the side his head came out (White's left). Here, he attacks the arm on the same side as his head (White's right).

Even if you miss the submission off the sit-out, it is a simple matter just to roll over and attack your opponent's back, provided you are able to drive him down with the sit-out. Either way, make sure to get your head out far so that your upper back presses into your opponent's side as you sit out and drive them down.

Blue attempts the technique from the top of page 198.

As he begins to sit out, White pulls his arm free.

Blue must keep a tight hold on White's elbow.

▲ Blue leans back into White's back/armpit. Blue puts his right arm over White's back, both to control White and to help himself adjust his weight.

Blue will not be able to re-grip White's left arm, but he can get the right. Blue wraps his left arm around White's elbow and clamps it to his side.

Blue sits out.

Because White's arm is bent, his shoulder is torqued as Blue sits out. For this technique, Blue wants to come out perpendicular to White.

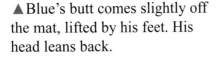
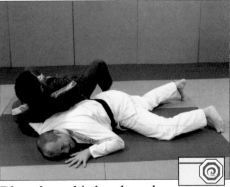

Blue's weight is concentrated on White's shoulder.

▲ Blue's butt comes slightly off the mat, lifted by his feet. His head leans back.

Blue clasps his hands and lifts White's wrist. The result is a shoulder crank similar to the *Kimura*.

🌀 Like the previous sit-outs, Blue posts on his a hand and the opposite foot. Unlike the previous sit-outs, Blue uses the his other foot and arm, relative to his head.

Blue's head is off to White's right side. Blue holds White's belt with his right hand.

As Blue sits out, his right hand keeps White's hips away.

As soon as he is on his butt, Blue posts his foot on White's knee. The back of Blue's neck pushes the back of White's right arm.

As White's chest goes to the mat, Blue brings his leg in front of White's face. His left shin replaces his left arm and continues pushing away White's face.

Blue uses both his arms to control White's arm. Blue's shin slides deeper under White's head.

Blue extends his torso and raises his left knee for an armbar. It is important to be aware of the way the opponent's elbow is oriented so you can pull the opposite way. Pull opposite the direction of their thumb.

With his foot still in place, Blue sits back, extending White in the process.

Blue wraps his inside (right) arm around White's right arm and places his palm on the back of his head.

With his other (left) arm, Blue pushes away White's head. This straightens White's arm. Blue's left knee pushes down White's hips.

White manages to prevent Blue from controlling his arm. Blue begins his counter by posting on his right elbow and reaching over White's back.

Blue brings his chest tight to White. He puts his left hand on White's shoulder.

Blue bases on his right elbow and uses his grip on White's shoulder to help himself throw over his left hook.

Blue puts his left arm on the near side of White's face and scoops White's forearm with his right arm.

Blue puts his left leg in front of White's face and uses both his arms against White's trapped arm.

Blue curls back his left leg around White's face while pushing down with his hips for the armbar.

Before Blue can sit out, White pummels an underhook.

If Blue tries the sit-out from here, he is likely to throw himself into a painful neck-crank.

Blue cups his hand behind White's elbow.

Blue drops on his right hip/side. His right arm pulls as his left arm lifts. It is critical when Blue drops back that he be on his side and not flat on his back.

Blue's left instep hooks White's leg and elevates. White's left arm is trapped, preventing him from posting on it.

Blue's roll continues with him tucking in his right elbow to secure White's left arm. Blue drives White's shoulder to the mat.

⊘ Use this sweep when your opponent stuffs the sit-out by pummeling an underhook. A key element, once again, is the position of the head. The head needs to be off to the side of the opponent's body. Blue does not carry White's weight on his neck; it goes on his shoulders.

Blue must switch direction. His right knee begins to drop as his weight goes to his left knee.

Blue drops to both knees. His right knee is directly under him. Blue's head is somewhat out to White's side. Blue's neck presses into White's armpit.

Blue's free arm wraps around White's thigh from the inside. Blue places his left foot between White's legs and drives forward. White will push back in reaction.

Once he feels that White is at the point of no return in terms of being swept, Blue lets his hook go and concentrates on moving to side control.

As Blue comes to his knees, he will remove his head from the side of White's body and immediately transition to side control. As Blue transitions to his knees, he continues to hold White's arm, keeping White's shoulder pinned and preventing escape.

Blue is in side control. With the grip he has with his left arm, he needs to be wary of White pushing on his head and trying to get an inverted triangle.

Back-roll & Turtle

► **Back-roll:** Look away from the shoulder you roll over. Roll on your shoulder, not your neck. Post on a hand and opposite foot as you sit through back to guard.

► **Back-roll:** When an opponent is involved, your head must come out to one side in order to complete the rotation.

turtle attacks

► **Double-leg 1:** Once your feet come over to the mat, lunge forward with your shoulder and wrap up their knees with both arms. Drive forward, then run your legs over theirs: side control.

► **Double-leg 2:** This time, the head comes out to the other side and the inside of your face drives into their side while you scoop together their knees.

► **Turtle Arm Drags:** Hold their arm tight to your own chest (you can also do this move with your other hand holding their arm). Once you are on top you can switch to side control, or....

► **...continue to Americana:** Keep control of their wrist as you reverse the scissor legs moves that you used to turn them over. Use a figure-four grip to get the Americana.

► **Sit-out:** Pick a side and get your head off to that side while sitting out, throwing up your outside shoulder as you do. Keep circling to their back.

back roll attack

► **Sit-out-armbar:** Attack the arm on same side as you sit out. Trap that arm in your armpit and slide your back on top of their shoulder. Clasp your hands and lift up their wrist to pressure their shoulder.

► **Armbar from the side:** Sometimes when you back-roll to guard, your head ends off to their side. If so, consider attacking the arm behind your head.

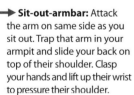  

► **Kneeling fireman's:** Use this if they under-hook from over the back of your head. Make sure you are on your side, not your back, as you sweep them.

CHAPTER 11

FROM THE GUARD TO THE KNEES OR FEET

The rules of Brazilian jiu-jitsu discourage abandoning a ground-fight for a standing fight. BJJ is, after all, a ground fighting discipline. Regardless of the wisdom of that approach, there are many reasons not to stay in the guard position. In competition, you might judge that you are better off not being in the guard either because your guard is weak or your opponent's guard passing is strong. Perhaps you prefer to be on top, or maybe you prefer to play for the take down. In a self-defense scenario, you need to be concerned with the possibility of multiple assailants. In a mixed martial arts contest, you might prefer to stand and strike. Whatever the situation or your inclinations, your game is not complete if you do not have techniques for getting to your feet. This being a sport-oriented volume, the techniques here do not involve giving up contact with the opponent completely, though it should be obvious how one would disengage were that one's objective.

This chapter shows techniques built off of two similar snake moves: the snake move to the knees and the snake move to the feet. Both snake moves use the same core body movement, and it is a simple matter to switch from the knees to standing and vice versa. In some of the photos, you will see that Prof. Moreira goes to one knee and one foot, something midway between the two techniques. Whatever the case, you first need to make space between yourself and your opponent. Sometimes your opponent makes it for you by backing away, and sometimes you need to make your own space by pushing away his hips with the soles of your feet. There always needs to be space between your upper bodies before you snake to the knees or feet.

Once you are out of the guard, do not be content with just getting off the mat. If you attack right away, you should avoid any sort of penalty in a BJJ competition. More importantly, you will keep your opponent on the defensive. Look for opportunities to push your opponent's head down and attack from there or to loop a collar choke, which are the types of attack shown in this chapter. Both tactics are easier if your opponent is bent forward and your head is higher than his, so elevate. But be cautious when standing that you do not give your opponent an easy opening for a single or double-leg take-down.

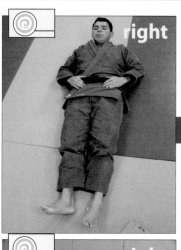

❷ Blue comes up on his palm and opposite foot. As he pulls his bottom leg under, his upper body is counterbalanced by his lower body. As his head moves forward, his leg moves backward. Once he gets to a knee it is time to either stand or attack.

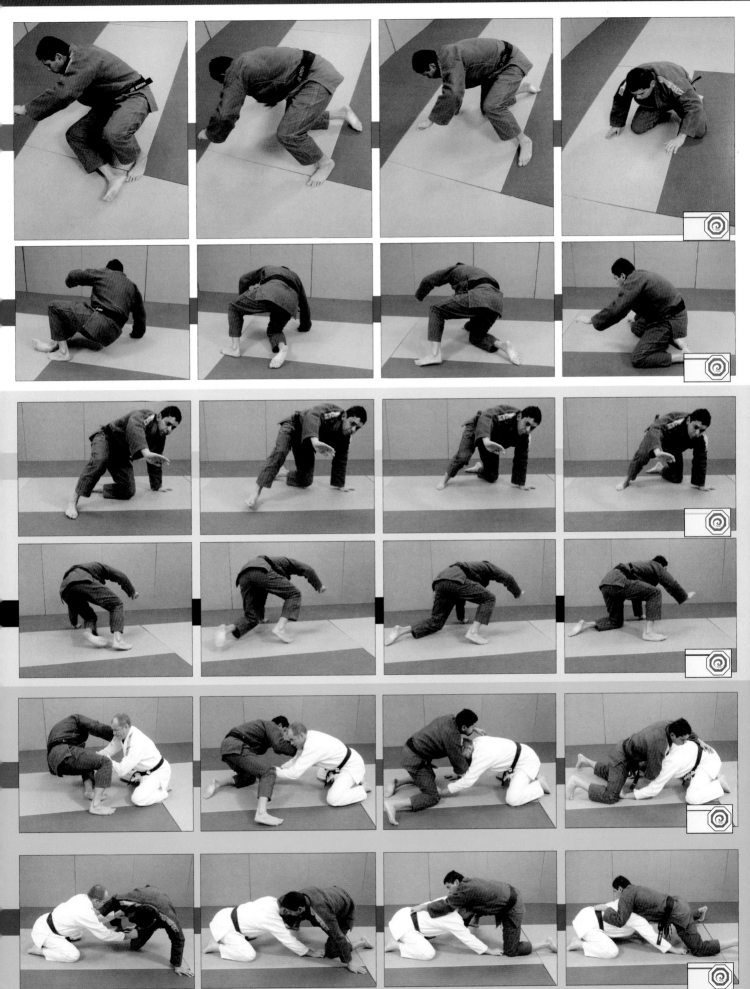

In a combat situation, it often takes more than just one hip movement to get to where you need to go. As you retreat, your opponent is likely to follow. As long as you can improve your position incrementally, you have a chance to succeed.

Here, Blue makes a first snake move to make space so he can straight-arm White. Once he does, he is then in a position to use his snake-to-the-knees technique to complete his escape.

White is in side control. Blue is better off if he begins his escape before White can tighten control. Blue posts his right foot and puts one hand on White's hip and the other on White's collar bone.

Blue turns to his side and moves his hips away from White using the basic snake move.

As White follows, Blue deflects the pressure so that White's torso lifts. Blue turns slightly to his back in the process.

Instead of going directly to his palm, Blue makes a small hip movement from his elbow.

Now Blue has the space he needs to base on his palm.

Blue's bottom leg moves in an arc underneath him.

Blue scoots his hips back a little more as he turns into White again.

Blue pulls his left elbow back, tracing an arc. His right arm is straight and braced on White's collarbone.

At this point, Blue will put his weight onto his right foot and left elbow, taking it off of his hips.

Blue's foot stops well behind him. Blue puts his arm on the back of White's head.

Blue pulls White's head down...

...and controls White's head by leaning into it.

This is similar to the first technique of this chapter. The principle of counterbalancing is the same. Here, however, Blue comes to his feet. This is a very useful technique for standing up in a self-defense or *vale tudo* situation.

Blue posts his foot.

He comes up on his opposite elbow.

He comes up on his palm and transfers his weight to his posted hand and opposite foot.

▲ ▼ In a sport jiu-jitsu context, the opponent will often try to hold your gi near your knee. This technique generates enough momentum that you should have no problem breaking that grip, provided you put a little snap into the movement of your leg.

As Blue's bottom leg moves back between his posted hand and foot, his head comes forward. This way, his head and leg counterbalance each other.

Blue keeps his free hand in front of him to ward off his opponent.

Blue stands, ready for whatever comes next.

As Blue comes up...

...he pulls White down.

Blue keeps White bent over by grabbing the back of White's neck.

Blue's chest drops on White's back.

❷ The most obvious use of the snake move to the knees or the feet is as a defensive measure or means of escape. But you can use it offensively. As you snake out of the guard and to your knees or feet, your opponent may try to lean into you. If he does, he will fall forward into the space you just vacated. Use that moment to pull down the back of his head and attack. Here, Blue uses the moment to take White's back. He has many options, as we will see in the pages ahead.

White pushes Blue's knee down but has little control of Blue's hips.

Blue straight-arms White, comes to his elbow, and pushes himself away using his right arm and right foot; his left foot blocks White's knee.

Blue goes to his palm.

White has compromised his base by following Blue. Blue capitalizes and pushes White's head down.

Blue's hand alone won't be enough to keep White down. He immediately places his chest on top of White's head and shoulders.

Blue takes a big step with his left foot, moving it under his right leg. It is very important that he keep weight on White's back from here on. Note how he positions his right arm as he steps over.

Blue's right foot was near White's left foot. Blue has stepped his right foot back to the outside of his butt, ready to spring.

Blue uses the technique for the last spread. It is okay if Blue bends his arm at this point; he has all the space he needs and does not want to stuff his own movement.

Blue pulls his leg back with authority so there is no way White can hold on.

Blue's right hand takes White's right lapel.

Blue takes a big step with his right leg and brings his right hook over and in.

Blue secures his other hook (not visible), taking White's back.

◉ Any time you can force your opponent to his hands and knees, the *clock choke* is a possibility.

White is protecting against chokes by bringing his chin to his chest. With his right hand, Blue pulls down on White's right lapel so that he can feed it to his other hand.

In order to get his hand under White's chin, Blue grinds his knuckle just below White's jaw line. Note the shape of the hand.

White's head is twisted slightly as Blue's hand comes under his chin.

First Blue shuffles his feet forward...

...then he steps his trailing leg under.

Blue presses his right hip down on White's left shoulder while at the same time pulling up on White's lapel. Blue's forearm levers off his hip, and the twisting of his torso generates force to the pull of his arm while at the same time making the choke tighter by pushing White's shoulder down.

Blue's right hand feeds the lapel to the left hand.

Blue must constantly keep weight on White's back during the transition that follows.

Blue moves his weight over White's head.

↻ Use the power of your body's core by dropping your hips down as you pull up.

The pressure from the hips forces White's shoulder down. At the same time, Blue puts his back into the pulling/choking action of his arm. Blue keeps his right arm tight to his body as he twists his body. This way, the power of his twisting is transferred to his arm. The choke is powerful because it combines gravity and torso strength.

Blue blocks White's knee with his left foot. Blue's straight right arm has transitioned to a fingers-in/thumb-out lapel grip.

Blue bases on his left hand and brings his right foot back, sole of the foot on the floor.

Blue uses his snake move to go to his knees. As he does his forearm comes under White's chin. White loses his base when Blue retreats.

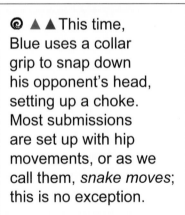

> ◉ ▲▲ This time, Blue uses a collar grip to snap down his opponent's head, setting up a choke. Most submissions are set up with hip movements, or as we call them, *snake moves*; this is no exception.

> ◉ Here is a look at the action of the arms during the choke. Blue uses the back of one hand against his other forearm. The pressure of one arm against the other draws both tighter.

Blue and White are postured for purposes of demonstration.

Blue pulls down on White's right lapel, forcing White to drop and post his hand out for base.

Right away, Blue pushes down on White's head.

Blue slides his arm across and lowers his weight for the choke (see below).

As Blue's arm slides across the back of White's neck, the back of his hand presses against his own forearm.

Blue uses the back of his hand as a leverage point, and with it he is able to exert extra force into White's neck by lowering his left elbow.

The choke is brought into full effect as Blue pulls the lapel, levers down his forearm, and pushes his chest into White's back.

Blue takes a deep lapel grip, and as he goes to his knee, he brings his forearm across White's throat.

Blue puts weight into the elbow that pushes down White's head.

Blue rotates his forearm under White's head as his shoulder and biceps continue to control White's head. Even as he rotates his arm under, he never lets the pressure off White's head.

❷ This is a continuation from the technique on the last spread. Here, Blue is at first unable to finish the choke. White tries to escape by moving his head off to the side. Blue follows up right away by cross-facing White as a means of setting up another choke.

❷ During the technique above, White defends Blue's choke by lifting away Blue's outside (left) elbow. No defense is without a weakness. Pulling off Blue's elbow creates an opening for Blue to loop his arm around White's neck and hit a choke from another angle.

Blue attempts the previous technique.

Blue moves White's head out to Blue's right side.

Blue posts his left hand.

Once again, hand and opposite foot.

Blue reaches across to grab White's shoulder.

Blue pushes his left biceps into White's head, causing it to tilt away from Blue. He pulls on White's shoulder not because he wants it to move, but for leverage.

Blue's left hand is pulling on White's right shoulder, pushing the side of White's head with his bicep and pushing his weight forward. This causes White's head for bend into the collar choke, making it worse. Blue's right hand pulls White's lapel tight. Blue pushes his chest forward for the finishing touch to the choke.

White pulls off Blue's elbow to defend.

Blue moves his chest over White's head.

Blue's left hand shoves White's head.

Blue swings himself back under, securing a loop around White's neck in the process.

White is pulled forward from his neck.

Blue scoops White's arm and holds his own head. Blue's right foot stops White from moving forward to ease the choke. Blue leans back to stretch White out to finish the choke.

❷ Here is another possible entry into the previous technique. This time, instead of trying to finish the loop choke from the bottom, Blue stands up and then sits back, creating momentum for a sweep and the opportunity to finish the move from the top. Blue could make a similar sweep from the end of the last technique also. Since he would not have as much momentum going into the move, he would need to rely more on leg strength in lieu of the momentum he gets from dropping from the standing entry shown here.

This is an example of good posture for playing this sort of straight-arm-sitting-guard.

Blue uses the structure he has made with his arms to keep White away as he comes up on his opposite hand and foot.

Blue kicks his leg free of White's grip. White falls into the hole where Blue vacated space.

Blue underhooks White's arm and tilts White's body sideways.

▲ Blue steps his left leg forward, ready to hook White's leg. ▲ Then he swings his other leg forward preparing to sit back.

Blue spirals down. He lowers his butt so that it lands relatively close to White. His right leg is to the outside of White's left leg. Blue lands on his right side.

Blue snaps down White's head with a pull on White's lapel.

As Blue goes to his knees, White lifts his head. Blue raises his level accordingly so that he can push White's head down.

From a standing position ,Blue has a better angle for setting up the choke and more potential to use his weight.

Blue loops his arm around White's neck as he drops his chest onto White's shoulders.

Blue elevates White and rolls White over White's left shoulder. Blue falls to his side, not on his spine. Only one shoulder goes to the mat.

Blue will remove his inside hook right away.

Blue makes White feel his weight. He pushes off the balls of his feet.

Blue drops his hips, raises his shoulders, pulls, and extends his chest to tighten and finish the loop choke.

❷ This choke begins the same way as the last few. Blue straight-arms White and comes to his feet. White bases out with his right arm in an effort to fix his posture, but as he does, a big space opens up on his right side. Blue takes advantage of that space by ducking his head under it and clearing White's posted right arm in the process. You must commit to the entry for this technique to work well.

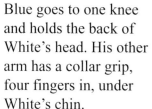

Blue goes to one knee and holds the back of White's head. His other arm has a collar grip, four fingers in, under White's chin.

Blue comes to both feet and loops his arm around White's neck. He moves his body more than he moves White's head.

Blue drops forward with White's head to his side. Blue's free arm scoops under White's right. Note that White's head is off to the side.

Blue ducks his head under White, through the space beneath White's armpit. Blue's head does not just go under, but also across.

If your opponent's ribs wind up smashing your head when you attempt this technique, you are not ducking your head under far enough. As you roll your opponent over, your head should already be somewhat to the front of his chest, not to his side.

Blue whips his right leg up and over. The impetus turns him over and tightens the choke. The back of Blue's hand, not the palm, goes behind White's head.

Continuing the rotation of his body, Blue's knees come up and over while he pulls down with his right hand.

Blue will roll all the way to his belly. As he comes over, his left arm will slide under White's head, ramping it up and making the choke tighter.

Executed properly, this is a very tight choke.

➋ The loop choke is a key component of the type of sitting guard shown in this chapter. If your opponent refuses to let go of your knee (Blue's left knee in the photos), or if they try to use that grip as base to circle around you, they will give you the opening for the loop choke.

Maybe Blue is unable to break the grip White has on his, knee, or maybe Blue lets him keep the grip with the intent of making the loop choke.

Blue creates space. His arm is straight, and he presses his knuckles into White's collarbone.

White lowers his head to counter the pressure from Blue's fist and to better push forward.

Blue drops his head to the mat as his left knee pushes into White's side, helping him rotate his lower body.

Blue moves his head under White. Blue steps his feet to lift his hips and rotate into the choke.

Blue walks his feet toward White's twelve o'clock. He blocks White's hip with his free arm.

💿 The loop choke is very effective, but it tends to be an all or noting technique. Either your opponent is going to tap, or you are going to wind up in their side control.

White circles to Blue's side. Blue sits up high and shoots his left leg out to White's side. If the choke fails, Blue's guard will be passed.

Blue commits to the choke. It's do or die from here. Blue lifts his elbow to make the loop around White's neck.

Blue throws his free arm across White's chest, under White's arms. He pulls the choke tight as he does.

The arm in White's hip stops White from turning along with Blue. Blue's head is under White's torso at this point.

As Blue continues to walk his feet and move his head under White, he also brings his right shoulder to the mat.

The farther Blue circles, the tighter the choke gets. If White tries to turn out of the choke, Blue will roll on top of him [*next page*].

◉ In the previous technique, White circled around Blue's knee, which he had pushed to the mat. This time, he pins the knee and drives forward into Blue. White then tries to block Blue's head with his arm. White's arm gets stuck as he circles his feet. As a result, White gets turned over.

As he attempts to pass, White drives his upper body at Blue. Blue is sitting up and has a collar grip. He pushes down on White's head.

Blue lifts his right elbow and sits into White as he guides White's head to the side.

Blue lies to his left side first, not his back.

Blue's left arm goes across White's body and holds near the armpit.

Blue turns to his right side and bridges a little to add power to the rotation.

White's arm is trapped, and as a result, he gets rolled.

Blue switches the position of his non-choking (left) arm. It will underhook White's right arm.

Blue's hip traps White's head in the loop.

Blue brings his hip in against the back of White's head. Blue's belly pressing against his own arm adds pressure to the pull of his arm. The result is a choke or a neck crank.

Snake Knees & Stand-up

@ *It is not always desirable to fight from the guard; consider backing away and to your knees or feet; be the one on top.*

Snake move to the knees: Base on your palm and the opposite foot. Your bottom foot traces an arc as the head comes forward. The upper hand protects.

Application: The upper hand posts into the collar bone as you move back, then pulls the lapel down as you pull yourself forward over their back.

Go to the back: If, when your chest gets to their back, their hands and knees are far apart, pivot off your chest and spin to their back.

Clock choke: If they lift their head up, you have an easy path across their neck for a lapel choke. The power of the clock choke comes from dropping the hips on their shoulder.

Choke from the front: If you already have a good collar grip as you get up, choke using that arm. The other forearm presses the back of their neck as you lever that hand off your other forearm.

Biceps choke: Keep the lapel grip. The other arm reaches across their face, grabs their shoulder and pulls the biceps into their face opposite the lapel pull.

Loop choke: They pull off your arm, your under-hook their arm as you bring your body around their head, looping their head within your arm. Sit back to tighten it up.

Loop choke sweep: If your opponent sits up, stand up. Put their head to the side and loop their head with your arm. As you sit back, use an inside hook sweep them to side control.

Loop choke, over and back: With the lapel grip in place, dive your head under their armpit. Pull with your arm as you roll. As you go belly down, your other hand goes over their shoulder and under their neck.

Loop choke: As they try coming around to your side, throw on the loop choke. You must commit to the choke. Walk your legs in a circle to tighten the choke.

Loop choke to neck crank: Blue continues to turn and is rolled over. Blue uses his hip to make pressure to the back of White's head for extra choking power or a neck crank.

⟳ Instead of attacking from the knees, you may prefer to stand. Once standing, you can use your take downs.

Snake to stand-up: Once again the key is to post on a hand and opposite foot. The lower body counterbalances the upper body as you stand up to a fighting position.

Application: If they are holding your knees, snap your bottom leg out to tear free of their grip. Use a lapel grip to block as you back out, then to yank them down, as you stand.

CHAPTER 12

SWEEPING A STANDING OPPONENT

In this chapter we go over a series of sweeps against a standing opponent. These techniques all begin with guard player's feet on the opponent's hips. From there, you have a number of options, as does your opponent. As hip movement is key to grappling, so is controlling your opponent's hips. If you can move their hips with your legs, you have a chance to off-balance them. As long as your feet are on their hips, they cannot pass your guard. So then, most of the time, when your feet are on their hips, your opponent's first move will be to do something to get them off. You need to expect that and be prepared for it.

If your opponent backs away while your feet are in his hips, you basically either have to follow them, or stand up. We saw technique for standing up in the last chapter.

Supposing you do not want to stand up, holding your opponent's sleeve ends is a good start towards keeping them from clearing your legs. But even with sleeve control, they will be able to move their hips and break contact with your feet. When your feet/legs lose contact, your opponent gets the upper hand. You need to re-establish contact (or stand up) before the situation deteriorates. One method for keeping your legs in contact is to hook that foot behind your opponent's knee. The first four techniques in this chapter all rely on hooking a foot behind the opponent's knee. Once you do that, you have a solid connection you can use for pulling yourself to them and/or them to you.

If your opponent is not actively trying to remove your feet from their hips, you can go on the offensive by moving your hips under theirs so you can lift their hips using the power of your legs. If there hips come up, so do their feet. Once you have their legs elevated, you have an advantageous position and sweeping them heels-over-head. The last three techniques of the chapter involve variations on the lifting the hips strategy.

❂ There are additional chapters on how to use the guard to attack a standing opponent at the Grappling Arts Publications web site: *www.grapplingarts.net*. Techniques include going from closed guard to submissions and sweeps, the spider guard, and single leg sweeps. Check them out; they are free if you have this book.

Blue has control of the sleeves and his feet in White's hips.

White leans back and begins to step back with his right leg.

White pulls free his right arm. As he does, Blue turns slightly to his right side and immediately hooks his left foot behind White's trailing leg.

🌀 Use this if they step back with one leg.

Now that White is falling, the role of Blue's sleeve grip changes. Once White is falling for sure, Blue can use the sleeve grip to help lift himself.

As White falls, Blue see-saws up.

▲ Blue can use his free hand to post. ▲ Or, depending on the angle White falls to, Blue can come up by a different method.

Blue uses his forward snake move to follow White (see pgs. 24-27).

Simultaneously, Blue scoots forward with the help of his palm on the mat, pulls with left hook/foot, and pushes with his right foot.

Blues right hand is just keeping White from grabbing anything. His legs make the sweep.

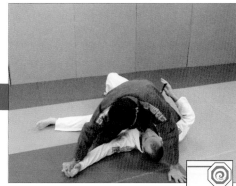

Either way, Blue uses his grip on White's sleeve to pull himself forward.

Blue brings his knee through the middle.

Blue ends in the mount.

❷ This time, White counters by pushing down on Blue's hooking left leg. Blue tightens his abs as White does so that he is better able to move his upper body forward. Thus, Blue uses the momentum White creates by pushing down against him.

White steps back to clear Blue's leg from his hip. Before he gets too far away, Blue hooks his foot behind White's retreating right knee.

Once the hook is in place, White cannot retreat without pulling Blue's leg with him.

White has a little control over Blue's knee, but none over Blue's leg below the knee. Blue's free hand either ▲ grabs behind White's calf, or ▲ grabs White's wrist.

Blue reaps White's left leg. He hits White's leg low, below the ankle.

As with the previous technique, once White is at the point of no return, Blue uses his sleeve grip to pull himself forward.

White pushes down on Blue's left leg, trying once again to get it out of the way.

Blue goes with White. Blue turns deeper to his right side than with the previous sweep. He crunches his torso forward as he does.

Blue chops at White's ankle with one foot and shoves into White's hip with the other.

Blue needs to get top position right away, before White can block with his right knee.

Blue goes chest-to-chest right away. As he does, he clears his leg before White goes to half guard.

Blue is chest-to-chest with White. Blue is in transition; he will quickly adjust to a more secure hold from here.

🌀 This time, White is wise to Blue's follow-up sweep and counters it by dropping his body Blue is ready with a third option.

White steps back.

Blue hooks White's leg.

White pushes down Blue's hooking leg, drops to his knee, and lowers his upper body for base. Blue gets to his side and on his elbow.

Because White has lowered his upper body, Blue only has to sit up a little to get the under-hook with his right arm. He comes up on his left elbow to do so.

Blue takes his foot off of White's hip, and hooks it under White's knee. Blue gives up the base on his left elbow and uses that arm to trap White's right arm where it is.

As Blue drops down, he turns to his side, not to his back. Blue elevates White with his leg while rotating with his upper body.

Once White's back hits the mat, Blue can slip off the hook with his right leg and put that leg to the outside to finish the mount.

If your opponent steps forward after you hook their knee, you have a chance to get your hips underneath theirs. Once that happens, it is *bon voyage* for them.

White has his hands on Blue's knees and is starting to step back. Blue is already starting to react.

White steps back and Blue hooks his left foot behind White's right knee.

Blue brings his upper body up and he turns to his left side. Most of his weight is now on his left side.

Blue pulls with his left foot and pivots on his left hip. Blue grabs White's knee.

This time, White steps back again to stop Blue from sweeping.

As White squares back up with Blue, Blue squares back up to White, only this time his hips are under White's.

Blue's hips are now almost straight under White's. This is very good for Blue. Blue holds White's sleeves.

Blue pulls White's arms as if to put them on top of Blue's head. As he does, his legs lift White's hips.

Blue holds White's sleeves so that White cannot post his hands out for base.

Blue does not just push up; he also projects his feet over his own head.

As White goes over, Blue can use his feet like hands to hold onto White and pull himself over.

Blue picks one shoulder and does a back-roll over it.

Blue uses the grip on White's sleeves to help with the back roll.

A sweep to a mount in one smooth motion!

❷ Here is another entry to flipping the opponent over your head from the bottom. The key here is to quickly slide underneath the opponent by simultaneously pulling on his sleeves and lifting yourself with your feet. Doing so unweights your back for just an instant and during that time you slide into position for the sweep. If you can get your back a little bit off the mat, that is even better.

Blue has control of White's sleeves. White knows that Blue has many options from this range and so he steps back both of his feet.

As White retreats he pulls Blue's shoulders up. White will need to lower his butt a bit for balance. The bend this puts in White's thighs helps Blue lift up his back with his feet/legs.

Here we see Blue in the process of sliding under. White's natural reaction is to stand up when he feels Blue pulling him down/forward. This helps Blue.

Blue now has his hips in deep.

From here it is easy to lift White straight up. Once he is in the air White has no base and it only takes a little pull to send him over.

From here Blue will back roll into the mount as on the previous page.

All at once Blue pulls back with his arms like doing a row and curls back his legs. The soles of his feet are on White's thighs. His goal is to make White carry his weight for a fraction of a second so that he can slide his hips underneath White's.

Counter and re-counter: so it goes. As players move, opportunities come and go, only to be replaced by other opportunities. Anticipating opportunities is half the battle. Because Blue knows White's likely defenses, he is ready to seize the opportunities they present as they arise.

Blue is about to use the previous technique.

White is aware of the sweep and is cautious not to let himself be off-balanced forward.

White drops his center of gravity...

... and hops forward to stuff the sweep.

At this point White is committing his weight to his rear.

Blue lets go of White's sleeves and grabs White's ankles.

Blue pushes with his feet and pulls with his arms.

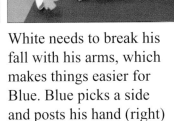

White needs to break his fall with his arms, which makes things easier for Blue. Blue picks a side and posts his hand (right) on the mat to the outside of White's leg.

Blue grabs a lapel with his left hand arm to pull himself up.

Blue hooks his ankles in under White's legs and takes the mount position.

Blue has control of both of White's sleeves, and his feet are in White's hips.

Blue hooks his left foot behind White's right knee as if to set up the *Open Guard Hooking Sweep* [pgs. 252-253]

White tries to push Blue's left knee down.

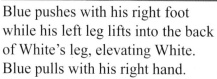

With his left hand, Blue can hold White's ankle ▲ or his sleeve ▲.

Blue pushes with his right foot while his left leg lifts into the back of White's leg, elevating White. Blue pulls with his right hand.

Even if White posts his right hand, he still has no base over his left shoulder.

Blue counters by circling his left foot to the front of White's body, though his knee stays stuck behind White's right leg.

By hooking his foot in front of White and pulling on White's sleeve, Blue nullifies White pushing on his knee.

With his foot still hooked in front of White's groin, Blue starts pushing his left knee into the back of White's right thigh.

Blue uses a grip on White's top (right) leg to help bring himself on top.

Blue's right leg comes back through White's legs and he hooks it around White's hips. Blue post on his right elbow.

Blue climbs on top, finishing in the mount.

Sweeping a Standing Opponent

⦿ *By standing, your opponent gains mobility but gives up base/stability. Use your legs to move their hips and take away their base.*

They step back: Use a forward snake move to follow them and hook their retreating leg.

They step back and hold your knee: Use the lumberjack sweep. Use the leg they are controlling to chop the back of their lead leg as you push their hip.

They step back and hold your knee and drop down: Under-hook their arm and with the foot in their hip to a hook under their leg. Control the hand on your leg and sweep.

They step back, then forward to defend: As they step back forward, your hips move under their. Lift with the soles of your feet, as you hold their sleeves. You have a flip-sweep.

Alternate entry to a flip-sweep: Pull both sleeves and use the soles of your feet to lift your butt. Pull your hips under theirs then hit the flip sweep.

They jump forward to stuff the flip-sweep: When they jump forward, let go of their sleeves and pull their ankles.

They shove your knee down: Before they get far, maneuver the sole of the foot of the controlled knee, into their upper thigh, then use that foot for leverage to lift into the back of their leg with that knee. Control their sleeve and push away with both feet.

Complete the trilogy!

Passing the Guard

The first book of its kind on Brazilian Jiu-Jitsu. The instant classic revised and expanded. *Passing the Guard* Demonstrates and explains in detail the range of skills and techniques needed to pass the guard. Widely regarded as the best book on Brazilian Jiu-Jitsu, *Passing the Guard* changed the way martial arts books and magazines are made.

Strategic Guard

Got defense? The first and only book to examine in detail the how to obtain, maintain, and retain the guard position. Over 2800 photos in 262 pages. Includes thumbnail flowcharts summaries, just like *The Guard*, and cross-referencing to *The Guard*. Detailed coverage of guard pass counters and submission defense for the guard player. Also includes offense, with chapters on sitting guard, and strategies on using the under-hook from the sitting guard.

Visit us at:

GrapplingArts.net

free downloads:
  extra chapters
  excerpts
  bonus material
  favorite techniques
  articles